"How does one locate and unlock the Middle West? I like to look for the inscribed grid of township squares, that checkerboard from above, sometimes punctuated with the Zen *enso* of a center pivot irrigation rig. Jim Reese, in this excellent and exacting collection, replicates that layout in many of these essays—topographies of stark juxtapositions, intricate quilted collages, high contrast and high definition chainmails of the Middle Border. Hopscotched and hobnailed, the pieces of *Bone Chalk* map out, again and again, the famous paradox of place where one is in the heart of the heart of the country at the same time one finds oneself in the middle of nowhere."

—Michael Martone, author of *The Moon Over Wapakoneta* and *Brooding*

"Jim Reese is an American original! His voice rises out of the Great Plains to bear witness to the foibles, folkways and oddities of living in the small towns and villages that are sometimes only a collection of a few dots of light to planes flying overhead in the dark. Reese has an easy voice to listen to—playful with a hint of deeper truths about the complex soul of the Midwest: dark and hopeful as we work hard to make lives in places beset by hard winters, hot summers, and constant economic uncertainty. Yet living here is full of humor and joy in the everydayness Reese chronicles with surprise and tenderness."

—Jonis Agee, author of *The Bones of Paradise*

"Like that longed-for drive down a Midwestern road, these brilliant essays introduce us to a startling diversity of people and places—rural and urban, wild and domestic, comic and cautionary. Our guide is the incomparable Jim Reese, whose wit and wisdom help us re-learn the value of listening, of loyalty and love and a good day's work. A writer who, as he says of his own beloved grandfather, is "a man more fully present and alive than most."

—John T. Price, author of *Man Killed by Pheasant and Other Kinships*

"In *Bone Chalk*, his first collection of nonfiction, Jim Reese brings the trademark honesty and humor of his poetry to the longer form, and the results are remarkable. His eye for detail and his empathy for those who live and work in the heartland is stronger than ever. He's still got his punch, direct and powerful, raw and refined. Whether he's looking forward or back, his vision is clear-eyed, laser-sharp, and full of heart."

—Jim Daniels author of *Eight Mile High*

"One of the beauties of Jim Reese's *Bone Chalk* is its invitation to the outsider to participate and to learn. Take, for example, "How to Become a Regular." Like Pauline and Linus Cummins, who "pause between bites of pie to see for themselves," the reader is asked to listen to locals playing euchre, "wide eyes showing all their white, hands hold five, no bid, Busch Light," to hear complaints about corn prices, to "laugh at the jokes," and, ultimately, to "talk about what you know." Throughout the book, we become familiar, as the author does himself—city kid from Omaha—with a unique landscape, culture, and people. Being a "regular" means being part of the small town and the surrounding rural community, knowing the stories and making stories. Reese doesn't write merely about assimilation, however; he writes about earned belonging to the habit of local, where there exists a "faith in all things that matter.""

—Mark Sanders, author of *Landscapes with Horses;* publisher of Sandhills Press

"Jim Reese is the chronicler of the back roads and broken down byways of America. He's in love with small-town palaver and High Plains hi-jinx. *Bone Chalk* is a true original."

—Brent Spencer, author of *Rattlesnake Daddy: A Son's Search for his Father*

"The physical distances between midwestern places like Omaha, Nebraska and Yankton, South Dakota are not that great, but the cultural expanses run wide and deep. In *Bone Chalk*, Jim Reese takes the reader into the profound vastness that defines the Great Plains. In this humorous and poignant memoir, the deepest recesses of the mysterious Heartland take on light, gain dimension, and rise into living color. Step onto Main Street, visit the local watering hole, drive the backroads to the farm, read the quirky bumper stickers of the Midwest, and watch empathy and understanding bloom with each new chapter. Love abides on every page of this wonderful meditation of place."

—Debra Marquart, author of *The Horizontal World: Growing Up Wild in the Middle of Nowhere*

BONE CHALK

Jim Reese

STEPHEN F. AUSTIN STATE UNIVERSITY PRESS

www.jimreese.org

 @ReallyhappyJim

Production Manager: Kimberly Verhines
Book Design: Ben Adams
Cover Image: "The Last Cornfield," Tristan Brewster

IBSN: 978-1-62288-203-8

For more information:
Stephen F. Austin State University Press
P.O. Box 13007 SFA Station
Nacogdoches, Texas 75962
sfapress@sfasu.edu
www.sfasu.edu/sfapress
936-468-1078

Distributed by Texas A&M University Press Consortium
www.tamupress.com

Contents

How many souls make up the inexhaustible winds?
How many of them taught with their bones' chalk?
What are the givens?

—from *Requiem for a Teacher* by Don Welch

How to Become a Regular

Picture Main Street. Pick-ups in a row like a used car lot, Chevy vs. rusted Ford. Tootie's Chicken full of farmers sitting at round tables, clean overalls and all. The stench of stale beer and urinals run dry. It's cards—euchre. Fists slam down on oak, the better the hand, the louder the bang.

See Pauline and Linus Cummins, two out-of-towners, pause between bites of pie to see for themselves. Hear Leroy Taverdy speak up every time an argument ensues. Leroy, the almighty authority on everything here.

Now, imagine, a more serious affair than prices dropping $2.00 a bushel. Edsel Thompson hollering, "There's more money in selling corn to Hy-Vee for lawn ornaments or decor than giving it away!"

Hear, "Open." "In." "Come on," at the euchre table. Loose change impatiently slides from one pocket to another. Lids squinting, pupils shifting and wide-eyes showing all their white. Hands hold five bid, no bid, Busch Light. Fists against the table. These tables on top of the floor. This floor covering foundation. This foundation, over the land they work.

Belly up to the counter and order a red beer. Grab the saltshaker and tap some on your napkin—it won't stick to your drink. Tomato juice and beer, who would have thought? Buy the guys at the bar their next round even if they have full drinks in front of them. Listen and laugh at the jokes. Talk about what you know if asked.

Later, as you get right with the world, ask Margaret Bender, the woman behind the bar running the show, "Can I get these fine ladies a drink when you get a minute?" Ask curiously and kindly. "Oh, young man," one of them will walk over and say while she reaches down and puts her hand on your thigh, "we aren't ladies."

Gaze at the thirty-seven stuffed animals mounted on these walls. 5x5's and buckskins over beer taps and booze. There are roosters on the run, two wide-eyed coyotes stopped in mid-dance, a full-breasted turkey fanning itself. Admire the large shadow box full of forty-pounds of Missouri catfish hooked on a stringer and polished with polyurethane.

Imitate the men leaning on the bar and swiveling on round stools in camouflage and Carhartt coveralls, all of them this evening immortalized amongst wildlife. It's been dark outside for at least four hours, but in here life illuminates. Hear the cackle and howl carry down Main Street, echoing call after call.

In one corner listen as Harold Tahatchenbach, blinder than a raccoon in headlights, bends the truth. "This big bastard today walks right under my godforsaken stand. Biggest buck I ever seen. And that damn rifle must have jammed or something and there I was stuck like a gopher in soft dirt." Listen to Harold, because everyone else does, because he's a nice guy. We all know he likely put more holes in the sky today than the lot of us. "That's alright, Harold, you old suck'n and buck," Leroy says, "You'll get him next time."

Watch Man Sits in Tree across from you, as he sips 45-cent coffee. He will laugh to himself for no apparent reason. Edsel Thompson, the guy next to you, talks too much. He will give you Man Sits in Tree's life story in five minutes. "Once," he says, "that crazy coot threw a couch on top of his trailer during a tornado to keep it from blowing away. Can you believe that?" Believe it, or pretend you do. "A person gets crazier and crazier every year of their life. You hear what I'm saying? You just hope it's a better kind of crazy. Right?" Laugh along. Try not to look sympathetic the next time you look at the guy.

Margaret will carry another plate of fried chicken to Leroy Lammers for a "thank you, ma'am" as he places a clean napkin in the neck of his shirt. Don't stare at Margaret's ass too long. It's hard not to, we all know it, but she's got eyes in the back of her head. Just play it cool. It's not just her looks either. Leroy really does live for this chicken. Try it, and when you do, eat more than one plate.

Edsel, your buddy now, plops another peanut into his rum and Coke and offers you some infinite wisdom about women. "She'd look real good underneath me," Edsel says. You've never seen anyone put peanuts in their drink. You remember your dad puts ketchup on his scrambled eggs, and you think that's weird, too.

Identical twins in their sixties, still dressed the same, stand patiently by the south door waiting for their booth to become free.

"Freaks," Edsel mumbles, as he turns to look over his shoulder. They are not any freakier than Edsel and his Planters peanuts, you think. Someday you'll have to introduce yourself and get their story.

Realize you will likely sit for a few more beers. Thank the other guys for ordering additional rounds. "I guess I have time for one more." Say it like that and don't forget to return the favor.

Watch Margaret fill the last of the salt and pepper shakers and throw her apron in the corner. She'll already have a few coming to her before you have a chance to order her a drink. Be cool, though, and offer her your seat. Go play a game of pool and maybe let the other guy win. Watch the evening fall away like it always does.

At last call finish your beer and leave your change on the counter. Laugh when Edsel tells you to keep it between the ditches. Wave goodbye to Margaret. Drive up Main Street, past the Service Station with its used tractor tires leaning against the garage and the flower shop with the miniature antique carnival carousel in the window spinning—the elegant horses moving up and down, illuminating the front of the store. See the last of the sinners stumble out of Ten Pin Lounge. Hear them holler and howl. Watch them take their last drags of cigarettes and stomp butts into cement. Don't stop. Go home. Feed the dog and drink another beer. Stare at the philodendron and make a note to water it in the morning.

MIDWEST Heartland/MID Heart WEST Land

I'm in the machine shed handing Carl tools as he rebuilds a 350 motor on his '76 Chevy pickup. "Always buy Chevy," he tells me. "Piss on Ford." Outside the door, salvaged cars, stray truck beds and parts accumulate in knee-high brome. The corncrib leans with the burden of a mortgaged crop. Blue tarps like bright military tents, perfectly aligned, cover a row of round bales and are weighed down with worn tires.

"I don't think this five-eighths is going to fit, Carl."

"Yeah. That's what she said."

There's an aura to Carl. At six-two, he demands attention. His face is sunburned and weathered. A painted sheen encircles his eyes when he takes his work glasses off. His hands are scarred from years of hard work. Carl gets things done. Plain and simple. I've never seen him start a job without finishing it. Carl may complain about work, but without it, he'd go mad.

"Hey bucket calf," he says, "we having fun yet?"

This is tough country, this Nebraska. It's unflinching and unapologetic. If you were to throw an ax at middle-America, it would stick here, in the Great Plains. The MID Heart WEST Land. It's the place we'd like to believe that keeps the working class honest. We've been given a lot of names—Midwesterners, Plainsmen, Prairie Schooners, Cornhuskers, Heartlanders, and Bugeaters. Like everywhere, banker's pockets swell off sweet deals while decent men's struggles run awry. Here, with everything spread out—where you can actually see the sky, piles of wealth and extravagance stand in sharp contrast to some families struggling to get by. A lot of the folks have been turning the dirt since they could first stand, continuing to work what their fathers and mothers left behind. Family profits fluctuating like the wind.

There is not a single definition that delineates the prairies. Common sense values such as physical labor, honesty in human relations, emphasis on the primacy of family and community, and intimate physical, emotional, and spiritual connections to the land are essential. When I first came here, I assumed those beliefs rang true for everyone, that Carl and his neighbors all inherited this land they work—honest rewards for sticking around. That's what a guy from the city believes. That romanticism of the small American family farm diminished in the late seventies and early eighties with the proliferation of corporate farming and American greed. It's nobody's business how many acres Carl owns or rents, or how many head of cattle he runs, and I've learned not to ask.

After another hour of fiddling with the motor, Carl decides we ought to go hunting on some minimum maintenance roads around the place. He grabs his Carhartt jacket—packs his Copenhagen chew, takes a dip. We are off.

Carl is trying his damnedest to pick off a ring-neck pheasant from the cab of another rusted-out Chevy when "Cat Scratch Fever" by Ted Nugent blasts over the airwaves, and he turns up the volume on his Kraco Deluxe stereo. The tweeters squeal and flush the remaining birds in the area into a thicket. Carl's singing crescendos to an out-of-tune home concert.

"Scratch that beaver—dear near near—scratch that beaver— bear nair nair nair!" This new rendition pleases Carl. Whatever sexual innuendos Ted Nugent has in mind will forever be lost for me on Rural Route 957, the image of Carl bending a guitar solo on his steering wheel now embedded in my brain.

"As worthless as tits on a boar!" Carl hollers over the remaining chords of the song as he mounts his shotgun under the .30-06 on the rear window rack.

"Screw it. It's beer thirty."

Carl reaches out and around the cab window to the bed for three beers. He shoves one beer in his breast pocket, tosses me one, and hammers back the other. He belches in mid-sentence.

"What?" I ask.

"Drink Budweiser and drive real fast. That should be their motto. Think about it. Why else do they have racecars on their cases of beer? Why do you think Dale Earnhardt, Jr. is their spokesman? If they didn't want us to drink and drive, they wouldn't put race cars on their products." He has a point. Carl could be the official spokesman for Anheuser Busch, Remington Firearms, or

NASCAR. I started drinking the Busch Light without thinking twice about it. But here in Cedar County things are a little different. Empty beer cans accumulate on the sides of roads and in pickup truck beds, common as dirt.

"You got farmers on one side tilling up every last shelterbelt and stand of trees, throwing up center-pivots. I might be one of the last guys in this county to think CRP is a good idea for the shit money the government pays me. There's not many pheasant left. Spraying herbicides and pesticides all over the goddamn place. I'd rather let a few more trees grow." He takes a breath and a long pull from his beer. "My back teeth are floatin'," he continues, pulling the truck over to take a leak. As he relieves himself, he points at something.

"Well, lookee here," he hollers to me from outside the cab.

"No thanks," I say, "I have a fine view from here."

"What? No. There. Look there."

On the horizon, Carl sees something. Off in the distance are rows of broken stalks. The combine's tires have made permanent ruts in this soil. About two-dozen head of Herefords are rooting in the field for leftover corn. The sun has begun its slow descent. The sky is bright orange, alive and on fire.

Since my engagement and moving to the country, what I've learned from Carl and men like him, is to really look. Some of us start out as just observers here. Not an inkling of what it takes to survive. I've never sat at the kitchen table calculating unforgiving ground—whole sections drying up at a time—families splitting up out of stubbornness and greed, going from breakdown to break away. Never felt this weather's heat or its twenty-below blows—at least not at first. And city folk, like me, who fly by on their weekend excursions, don't know unless they stop. And with time, you start to understand the heartland, this farmland, and its inhabitants. What keeps bringing me back to Carl, to this place, is its mystery. This country is a whole new world to me, and I try to get back here as much as possible. Each time I leave with a better understanding of what living is all about. Is writing a fit profession for a man? I don't know. But, I've always wanted to belong to these rigid places outside my comfort zone. I question my own existence and purpose in life every time I leave this new home of mine. Maybe I should be doing more. I look again into the setting sun, but see nothing.

"You're drunk!" I holler back to him.

"Drunk. Nah. I'm just getting started. Look up there on the north forty—at about nine o'clock. See that coyote? See that son-of-a-bitch?"

He jumps back into the pickup, and we're off. He grabs his CB, turns it to Channel 11 and makes contact. "The old man will hear us. He's always got this damn thing on. Harold you there?"
The old man he is referring to is Harold, a German farmer who fought in WWII—an old boy who never left the county since that call to duty overseas. Harold will take an old washer or dryer, or any metal object, grab his tin snips, and cut it up into one-inch squares for fun. Or, in between meals and chores, you might see him sitting on a feeder bucket, head over a rusted coffee can. In that can, he breaks up glass bottles. In a rhythmic movement, he quarter-turns an old rusted ball hitch, grinding the bottles into fine sand. When the can is full, he takes the remains and spreads them down the lane. Carl says he's creating his own glass highway. I sometimes wonder which way Harold plans to turn when he gets to the end of his lane.

"Yep," Harold's voice crackles back through static on the line. "Where you at?"

"Go up to Benson's gate and sit. I got an eye on one of those bastards. I'm gonna head over east of there and try and pick him off. I'll call you back in a few minutes."

The coyotes here have been tearing at the livestock. Both men have lost calves to this particular pack.

"I got enough goddamn problems without these mangy pieces of shit messing with my herd," Carl hollers at me as he guns the Chevy across the pasture. "Keep an eye on it if you can."

Humane or not, I'd kill the things, too, if they ate a potential $1,800 Hereford of mine. A man has to make a living. Out here, you try to live with wildlife the best you can. Most of the time it works pretty well. Other times Mother Nature and her tricksters remind us who's boss.

We blow across the pasture at full speed, hauling ass between sections and open gates. I grab the Chevy's passenger "Holy Crap" handle and press my back firm against the seat. Carl throws his beer can out the window.

"It works a hell of a lot better with someone on the other side of the section ready to cut the bastards off. Hopefully, the old man will get up there and stop him in his tracks," he hollers.

This animal is the predator and I'm easily on board to eliminate it—a normal and necessary means to an end. How did that happen? Why do I really care if we kill this coyote or not? Maybe, because I want to belong to this otherworld that has been foreign to city guys like me. Fighting for my space, my turf, makes sense. I know Carl well enough that he isn't going to just shoot something for the fun of it. There's a reason. Carl has to balance stewardship of the land with his own survival. He learned to hunt as a child—the safety and necessity of it, genuinely understanding animals and the hierarchy of what survives and thrives. Isn't that a learned trait for us all, though? How in our culture, whether we like it or not, success is often ingrained with the taking.

Where I come from—urban middle-America, Omaha, with apartment buildings and rows of split-level houses, manicured lawns and mega-malls we don't worry about coyotes. House cats are prominent, as well as dogs behind chain-link.

The animals and predators of my childhood were other human beings. *Never talk to strangers.* Those four words drilled into me since I could stand. When the serial killer John Joubert moved to Omaha and volunteered as a Boy Scout troop leader, and then started to lure and torture young boys—eventually kidnapping and killing two kids in the same part of the city where I lived—he was the predator everyone was after. I will never forget the police crime sketch on milk cartons and plastered to street poles—Joubert with his mirrored sunglasses and hoodie pulled tight around his head. It was my neighborhood, and we wanted it back. It was the paranoia of the eighties in Omaha.

In the blink of an eye I lose the coyote. I'm not sure I ever saw it, to be honest. This inimical speck of life, this coyote, vulnerable but elusive. What I'm looking out for now are rocks and holes. At the crest of each new hill, I see sky and feel my gut rise.

"I think my back teeth are floating now too," I holler back to Carl.

"Hey. Don't worry. I've been hunting this land since before you had hair on your balls."

"That's comforting," I holler back as we hit a rock and my head bounces against the roof of the cab. He guns the Chevy over the crest of the hill and suddenly slams on the brakes—my head and hands smash into the dashboard. "Damn!" I holler as my head finally comes to rest in the palms of my hands.

Carl spots the faint-gray coat of the coyote at the bottom of the bluff. With his binoculars, he points in its direction. I see something tan and yellow moving.

"You got an eye on him yet?" Harold squawks through the CB airwaves.

"Hot damn! Got him."

He hands me the binoculars and puts two cartridges in his rifle. He gets out and takes aim over the cab of the truck. My adrenaline is still on full throttle as I try to bring the coyote into focus, but my hands are entirely too shaky from the ride. I stare out the passenger window and begin opening the door as slow as possible. I hear him fire and pop up to see for myself. I stand up with my feet still inside the cab of the pickup and lean on top of the passenger door frame searching for the dead coyote.

Off in the distance, I can see Harold's truck, but struggle to see the coyote. The wind has picked up. Standing here on the running board of Carl's truck, trying to hold ground, I think how small we really are in the whole scheme of things. Harold's no bigger than my index finger from here. I squint to try and get a better view.

"Hey!" Harold screams through the CB inside the cab. "What are you waiting for?"

Turning around to see what Carl's doing, I come face to face with the dark end of his rifle.

"Don't—ever—do—that—again," Carl says it slowly and seriously, in a low voice. "You about got your head blown off. You don't even know what could've happened."

I am standing there, hanging on the passenger door of the truck, right in the line of fire, the rifle still laid across the top of the cab and pointed at me.

I can't say a thing. Although I have not been shot, I feel the numbness of a fired gun. I think hair-trigger. See myself in the crosshair. I am caught between predator and prey. I can hear my blood pounding in my veins. I turn away and spot the coyote. It paces back and forth a few times, then runs for cover. I'm stunned, unable to move. The wind whistles white noise.

The Mother-in-Law Archives

Year 1 Pre-Engagement

When I visited the farm for the first time, she prepared a tender roast with all the fixings for supper. Beef, potatoes, gravy, onions, carrots and corn. We mashed the potatoes with our forks. Slopped up the leftover gravy on our plates with white bread.

On Saturday, for dinner, we had roast. Beef, potatoes, corn, more bread. Does it always taste better the second day? Someone sliced a tomato. Two of us shared a few spoonfuls of gravy. That night, for supper, we had it again. The beef and what was left of the bread, mashed potatoes with butter and a jar of applesauce. We chewed and chewed.

Sunday, thank the Almighty Lord, we tackled some hocks of ham.

Just Married

My mother-in-law, the keeper of all things whole and necessary, puts leftover food in little plastic baby food containers and yogurt cups she has saved. Will leave half a chicken wing for someone else to eat. Wraps up and refrigerates one slice of bacon. Puts lemon juice on half an apple so it won't turn brown. Has a drawer full of mustard, barbeque, and soy sauce packages from take-out restaurants from out of town.

She cuts coupons. Cuts up and collects newspaper articles if she knows someone in the article or knows someone who knows the person in the article. Gives me play-by-plays of garage sales and auctions. Saves fresh scraps for stray cats—bones for the dogs. Saves for Jesus and saves for you.

Picks green tomatoes before the first winter freeze. Wraps them in tissue paper, serves them for Thanksgiving dinner. Balances soap dispensers upside-down like others do with ketchup bottles and eventually combines them in one bottle. Has a room full of old jeans in case her husband's overalls need patching, or her son-in-law's crotch blows out. Makes pie crust from lard (the only way to make pie crust). Has full canning jars from the '80s. Has unidentifiable things in her deep freeze. Once I saw her pull a tarp for a pick-up bed out from underneath her dresser. "I've been holding on to this, I don't know how long."

If you need something—a blow torch, nunchucks, twist-ties, marbles, propane, a chandelier, suspenders, a curtain rod, spare tire, a putter, basin wrench, bell bottoms, a bowling ball—anything; she's your woman.

Year 3—Honeymoon's Over

As we are blanching asparagus, I cut the hard stalk off and throw it on a pile for the blue heeler. I take the better half and toss it into boiling water. My wife and mother-in-law are watching a self-help video on some new cockamamie scheme that doubles your money in thirty days—guaranteed. I cut a fat stalk in half and holler over the noise of the television about making double. I layer those two pieces on top of each other and cut again. I yell to them about quadrupling. I continue to cut more and more, smaller and smaller pieces until my pile of asparagus forms its own mountain of green. They pay absolutely no attention to the dog or me.

Year 6 ½

My mother-in-law sends me detailed reports about Plantar Fasciitis, the weather, a neighbor's tumor, and family feuds. Although I only live about a mile from her and we see each other frequently, she still sends me group emails... "I had a cortisone shot in my heel last Friday for the Plantar Fasciitis. The heel pain is gone. Just hope it doesn't come back. I went to the J.C. Penney watch repair department today. They didn't have links to match my watch, but the clerk will order some and send them to me. I can fix it. I'm not paying someone to do it. It was a perfect day today, but ice and snow is coming tomorrow."

Once I emailed her and asked what it was like to be married to a farmer all these years. I expected one of her long emails, something that I could put in my book about the Midwest so I'd get a better understanding of things—a perspective from a woman who was born during the Great Depression, a generation that struggled and sacrificed to make ends meet. She never responded.

Year 9

My father-in-law and I are eating dinner—Swedish meatballs, potatoes, corn and bread.

"You won't believe this," my mother-in-law says. "But I found a container of cherries in the deep freeze that I froze in 1978. They still looked good. So I made a pie out of them."

"We've been eating it and haven't got sick yet," my father-in-law says. "That's the gospel truth."

"There wasn't a lot of freezer burn on them?" I had to ask.

"Some, but not that much." And she shows me the container the cherries were in. She dates and labels everything in the deep freeze. The masking tape is yellowed, the writing worn and barely readable. "And you cannot write about this or tell anyone who I am until you try a piece for yourself. That's the deal."

"Bring it on."

She reaches into the freezer because she has already frozen the pie; she doesn't want the leftovers to go to waste. She thaws two pieces in the microwave. My father-in-law digs into his piece.

"Are you sure it didn't say 1998?" I ask.

She smiles as I dig in, too.

Year 10½

7:45 at night, the girls are dumping bath water on each other and the floor. The phone rings and I pick it up. "Are you getting the girls to bed?" my mother-in-law asks.

"Yes, and I'm picking up this Christmas tree that just fell over."

"I bet you maybe had some help with that. Say, did you get that car key in the mail? The flyer says if your winning number matches the number on the mailer, then you could win one of four prizes; a new car or truck, even. I don't need a truck, but I could use that car. And my numbers match. Did you scratch your numbers off?"

"No. It's in the recycle."

"Okay then, I'll let you go. I just wondered if I should drive up to Yankton and see if I'm really a winner."

"No, no. Wait a second. I'll go check." I rummage through old magazines and paper and find the key to my new car. I scratch off a gray circle and pick up the phone: "Here's my winning number: 931418."

"Oh, hell, it's a scam," she says. "We both can't be winners."

Year 13

As I was walking across campus to teach, I kept feeling a sharp piercing on the inside of my thigh, like multiple bee stings, in places bees shouldn't be. In my office, behind a locked door, I pulled my pants down to check what the hell was going on. It was then I found a sewing needle in the crotch of my newly hemmed jeans. I was troubled. Not for the business that had gone unharmed, but for my overall well-being. My mother-in-law had done the sewing. I could only hope senility had set in and made her oblivious that she left a sharp needle here, of all places—but she doesn't forget. An instinctive shriveling rendered my jeans somewhat roomier than I remembered.

Year 15

"Guess where I put my potatoes?" the anonymous woman asks, dropping off a box of FFA potatoes at our house. "Twenty-six dollars for about ninety russets, and they are in my dryer. It's fifty degrees in there."

In my mind, I see her burrowing through a junk drawer to find a thermometer that still works. This in the home of a family deeply concerned with how hot or cold a room should be, how to appropriately insulate and save, how to overheat and suffocate company. I imagine the anonymous woman placing the thermometer in the dryer. Waiting, re-checking again and again until she's certain this is just as good as digging a big hole out back or placing them in the cellar she no longer has since they moved to town.

"You trying to invent some kinda slow-cooker, or a new way to make mashed potatoes?"

Once more, the anonymous woman looks at me with withering calmness, that of a practical person confronting the ditzy and incompetent.

Year 16

My father-in-law drives her to our house. He sits in his favorite rocking-chair he has given us and watches our 46-inch high definition television. The woman with him wants me to take her shopping. She has been comparing prices, like she always does, for more than a month. She wants me to help her pick out the right weed-whacker. "Those knees of his have been bothering him something terrible. I've been doing all the mowing."

She thinks I know a little more than the next guy when it comes to purchasing these things. I appreciate that, and I am not taking this task lightly. To be honest, I already have one picked out. A 29cc 4-Cycle Straight Shaft Trimmer. I know she won't go for it. It's the top of the line and more power than she needs. But, I have to at least try.

We visit the first store. She has trouble lifting the one I have chosen, so I don't push the issue.

The eager salesman is bombarded with questions for nearly twenty minutes until he excuses himself to use the restroom. We visit the second store. A mega-mart and no one is around to help. We visit the third store with over fourteen weed-whackers to choose from. We compare lithium batteries to plug-in trimmers, extended warranties and prices, prices back to warranties, plug-ins back to battery life.

"Well," she says, studying the *Yard Man* and its curved shaft trimmer—no oil and gas mixing, EZ Start for comfort and convenience. "I like this one. Good warranty. Should last me 'til I'm dead."

Year 17—Real Mayonnaise

This morning, early, their youngest daughter, my wife, rushes from room to room, plugging in the iron, checking the time. Staying home, I'll get the girls to school and back; I can't miss work. That's my excuse.

My father-in-law will wear his black work shoes, the ones with the thick soles, the only ones he still feels comfortable walking in. He'll grab his nicer cane that he keeps next to his bed. My mother-in-law will hem and haw over a blouse and the right color slacks for the three-hour drive, to the funeral in the city, with their daughter at the wheel. That my mother-in-law will bring along a road map and a plastic hand-held compass comes as no surprise.

When my wife returns from the trip she knows about everyone in town who now has a condition. Says she received a detailed report about every noise in their car and where it's coming from. Tells me how her dad interrupted and gave the play-by-play of farmers in the field planting too deep.

"When we stopped for gas, Dad said, 'just give me ten minutes to get outta the car.'" She smiles at me and then hands me a bag of sliced ham on cocktail buns spread with butter and real mayonnaise that her mom packed for the journey and no one ate.

Year 18

"It looked like everyone enjoyed what you said during Jack's eulogy. But, I couldn't hear a thing. My hearing-aid battery went out. You'll have to give me what you wrote so I can read it," my mother-in-law said.

Year 19—Good Company

The masking tape above the doorbell reads: *Please Ring Twice or Knock or Yell!* This faith in good company is what I admire in my mother-in-law. Faith in all things that matter.

Year 20—My Mother-In-Law and the Manhunt

NIOBRARA, Neb. --A police officer has been assaulted at the low-income housing units while attempting to arrest a suspect on a warrant. The suspect was able to disarm the police officer and point the handgun at the officer before leaving with the gun on foot into the river bottom area along the branch of the Niobrara and Missouri river.

I'm driving my mother-in-law to the eye doctor for laser treatment. We talk about preceding presidential elections. Gun control. Bi-partisanship. I make no jokes. She gives me no stares. She says, "I read in the paper that fella they're after is 5-10, 150 pounds. He's not that big of a guy." She's a farmer's widow now, born in the Dirty Thirties, when desperate people must have seemed almost common.

"I had a dream about him last night. That he showed up at our place." We look out at the dirt road before us, ruts veering towards the ditch as we crest a hill.

"I told him, you can come in and sit down. If you put that gun away, I'll fix you something to eat."

MIDWEST BUMPER STICKERS
A Retrospective I.

I LIKE CATS. **DEAD** ones.

Cherry County Nebraska has more momma cows
than any other county in the United States of America.

Why is what we've been doing for over 200 years
suddenly unconstitutional?

NUKE THE WHALES

My long-distance provider is Black Hills Ammunition

My peace sign is a cross hair

Buy a Gun Piss Off a Liberal

If you think passing a law
banning all guns is the answer...
criminals DONT pay attention
to laws DUMBASS

The second amendment is in place in case they ignore the rest

GOD GUTS GUNS

Made US
Free

Born in a Camper
Raised in a Cave
Hunting N' Camping
is ALL I Crave

My Other 4x4 Has Legs

I love animals,
they are delicious

I like my women like my deer: **HORNY**

I can muck 30 stalls before breakfast!
What can you do?

MORE COWBELL

Lock 'em and Drop 'em

If you don't like whiskey, huntin' and strippers, **don't
come here**

Keep Honking, I'm Reloading

Save a Cow, Eat a Vegetarian

ALARM = Mastiff

My horse bucked off your honor roll student!

Fishing stories told here. Some true.

I was normal…
then I bought my first horse.

**Behind every good horse
is a human…cleaning up!**

Have You Hugged Your Hog Today?

I'M RETIRED GONE FISHIN'

GUN CONTROL Means Using Both Hands

This Year I Got a New Gun For My Wife. Good Trade
Don't Ya' Think?

IF IT FLYS IT DIES

Ted Nugent **B**ow Hunters – **A**gainst – **D**rugs
Charlton Heston
is MY PRESIDENT

BOYCOTT Veal

I LOVE BEEF

EAT BEEF The West Wasn't Won On Salad

Old Man George
and the Chrysler Sebring
(A Midwest Journal)

Day 1

George parks his Chrysler Sebring in my yard, the left side in the street, the right side on my fescue. I have to mow around the car. The passenger side mirror is missing. The custom chrome molding that accents the middle of the two doors has been ripped off.

"Whiskey dents," I say to my neighbor.

"Old fucker dents," he replies.

Day 2

I'm going to water the lawn. I ask George to roll up his windows. He's leaning against his car—which is still parked in my yard. I see the neighbor's out. He waves me over.

"Give thy water to thy neighbor. That ought to get rid of that old bastard."

(Later putting the sprinkler and hose away:)

"You know, I was watching you mow your yard the other day." George takes a drag from his smoke. "You shouldn't push your mower up the hill like that and then let it roll back to you. Hill's too steep. You're gonna slip. A friend of mine did that once and cut himself all the way up to his belly. He got caught underneath the blade of the mower and got cut here." He points his right index finger at his crotch. "You understand what I'm saying to you?"

Day 3

George's car is gone.

Day 4

George is back. He parks the Sebring in front of my neighbor's house. He walks across the street and leans against the hood of my car, which happens to be at the end of the driveway, and has a smoke. My neighbor texts me.

I see he's back.
What the hell is that guy smokin?

Day 5

George parks in his daughter's driveway across the street from my house. The driveway is easily 30 feet long. His daughter's place has a three-stall garage, a rare luxury on this block. He takes a closet full of clothes out of his trunk. All day long, he comes and goes— unloading his personal belongings. Once he's done, he parks the car in front of my house again. It's gotta be the tree in front of my house. The shade he's after.

Day 6

George parks the Sebring in his daughter's yard. Backs the thing right into an evergreen bush. Three tires in their front yard. The front left—hanging over the curb, in the street.

Day 7

All day long, that tire hangs off the curb.

Day 9

I mow again today. I don't let the mower roll back to me. I cut the grass on the hill, pushing the mower at an angle, moving slowly from one side of the yard to the other, until it is cut properly.

Day 10

"You know, I used to work for Western Union when I was younger—your age. I'd bike from Havelock to West O Street four times a day. Didn't have a car. Didn't need one."

Day 13

George is sitting on my front stoop, smoking. When he finishes, he gets up, walks up the street and back down and sits on the hood of his car. The trunk is open. He lights another cigarette.

"The way he pulls on those cigarettes, you'd think he was smoking pot," my wife says.

"Maybe that's it," I say. "We can blame it all on the dope."

Day 14

George and his daughter come out to inspect the car. She's raising her voice, but I can't make out what's she's saying to him from inside the house here. She raises her arms. George raises his arms—loose flesh flapping. She shakes her head and walks back to her house. George tries to shut the trunk, but it continues to spring back open. He sits on it. Smokes. Gets off. Springs back open.

Day 15

George is gone. His daughter now drives his car. So does her boyfriend.

Day 18

"Sorry about the old man parking in your yard," the boyfriend says. "It won't happen again."

Day 24

I think they may have done something with George. I'm not sure, but I think the boyfriend did it.

Day 26

"Are you still looking for him?" My wife asks. "You're worse than a junior high girl."

Day 30

George isn't dead! I see him over there on his side of the street, on his daughter's stoop, chain-smoking and putting the butts in a rusted coffee can. His car is nosed up to the garage door. He doesn't even look at the Sebring or come over to sit on my steps. What the hell?

Day 33

I move our other car from the street into our driveway, just in case George wants to park in front of my house again. His car doesn't move for five days. When it finally does, he's not driving.

Day 45

The oil slick in front of my house is slowly disappearing. It's going to be November soon. I haven't seen George for over a week.

Day 46

When the dryer is running at George's daughter's house, a cloud of hot air spills from the vent and hovers over and around George's car. The bushes shiver. Their side door porch light flickers on and off. The wind erupts underneath their weatherproof grill cover as if George himself could be trapped. A single piece of chrome from his car glints through the fog of the hot air, which continues to escape the house.

Day 49

The hood of George's car is up. It's beginning to freeze at night.

Day 50

The hood is still up.

Day 51

Still up.

Day 52

Down.

Day 53

It must be George's birthday. Folks are coming and going. Most bring presents. George comes out of the house with a new Nebraska Husker leather jacket. It's two sizes too big. He walks up the block, comes back and sits on my stoop. I take the trash down to the curb.

"Nice jacket," I tell him.

"Birthday present. And we're going out for steaks if they would get out here already."

"Happy birthday, George."

Day 61

There was an ambulance last night—or this morning, depending on how you look at it. Either way it was late. After 2:00. Sirens and the whole shebang. A fire truck came, too. The lights from the emergency vehicles stayed on for longer than I expected throwing shadows and colors on the neighbor's houses. The sirens cut off when they parked. They wheeled George out after about fifteen minutes. He was covered from feet to head with a blanket. They had him strapped to the gurney.

"I ain't dead!" I heard George holler. "Am, I? I ain't dead! I ain't pushing daisies up yet!"

All the Warning Signs Were Posted

Possessive dandelions. Snot-nosed kids blowin' snowball-seeds into a headwind. Then I come upon three plumber cracks bending over a '77 Vega, Old Milwaukee in each right hand, pocket-pool in each left. Florence Boulevard is full blown with Harleys and home-brew, glass packs and malnourished mufflers. People driving. People bath-tub speeding.

"Say, Sugar, you got somewhere to go or are you just going?" It's tube-tops and flip-flops, sidewalk stubbed toes—bare knuckle, and third-shift swing—Arnold's Bar for orange breakfast beers, rocket fuel gin, the finger stir and Family Feud.

My two best friends and I had heard about this place from a close friend and had driven one night to the opposite side of the city. We arrived. And just like the rumors, he was standing there on the side of the building. A skinny man, hustling. "Hey, Vernon," our friend hollered. Vernon walked over, took our money and returned five minutes or so later with a brown sack of liquor. We had land-ed. After a while, Vernon had us pick him up at his apartment. No need for him to stand at the corner if we were going to be regular customers.

Some nights, Vernon's wife, Felice, would be feeling loose, un-buttoning clothes. We'd chisel ice for our drinks out of an old plastic ice-cream tub long empty of vanilla and chocolate swirl. Summer heat was still sticking. Ice picks and iron fans—humidity and cling. Sitting on one of the kitchen's mismatched chairs, Felice would spread her legs wide and start icing her cleavage and lips. Vernon would plug in the turntable and start spinning forty-fives. Felice might grab one of us and try to lead us in dance.

"I got songs to bring it up," Vernon hollered. "And songs to take it down. Don't be taking advantage of my wife, you hear?" Before long, Vernon would drift off somewhere else, sometimes physically, looking for what he called his own ten-penny high.

"Some sugar is right through that bedroom door," Felice whispered one night, tonguing an ear. That was our cue to leave. We all thought about it on the long drive home. Some of us talked about it, some of us joked about it, some of us sitting in the backseat didn't say a word.

* * *

It's been ten years or so since I thought about Vernon. Almost twenty-five since we used to beg the guy to buy us beer when we couldn't. I got an email out of the blue from my best friend back then in high school, T. The guy who wouldn't even sit on Vernon's couch unless he passed out on it. In the email he wrote:

> *Hey, these shitbag car salesmen I work with don't believe*
> *we used to go to the Black Magic Inn and get booze from*
> *Vernon. Didn't you write about that one time? I remember*
> *reading it on the internet. If it's still out there send me a*
> *link. And if you make it back to Omaha, I'll buy you*
> *a beer. Or better yet, one of your Kamikaze concoctions.*
> *Check this picture out—place is still standing.*

You can Google it—the old red brick split-level where we'd sit out on the stoop and wait with Vernon for his monthly unemployment check. It was cut on the third of every month and in the mail from the state government that day. On the fourth and fifth, a group of them would be out on the stoop, waiting for Fred the mailman to deliver the goods. Fred came every day but Tuesday. Everyone knew Tuesdays was Fred's day off. None of the men standing on the stoop had steady work. Vernon would likely have a string of debt he'd accumulated from the prior month's sour offerings. "Everybody always wantin' something, Jimbo," he'd tell me. "Man's always taking. My girl wants to perfume the place up, and my daughter needs a trumpet for next year. Got to find me a trumpet. Hell, I know something. We got to eat—gotta get me my check."

"You gotta get your Skol is what you gotta get," Solly said. Solly came out of 1C wearing his girlfriend's bikini briefs and two different see-through dress socks. Some days, he came out to see for himself, if he was going to stand in line at the corner store to get himself some work. Maybe Manpower would give him another shot.

Or it might be just one of those days.

Clarence, who came from around back of the apartment, hadn't gone down to the corner for last month and a half. He walked up on the front landing, yawned, dug his hands in his shorts and scratched himself.

It was another strike on the stoop. Vernon, skinny as hospital toilet paper, would be bumming smokes from us and living off of everyone else's dole. He'd start getting itchy and agitated, looking down, picking up cigarette butts, relighting them—scratching at the backs of his hands.

"Maybe the man cut you off, Vernon." Someone always said it.

"I'm disabled. Can't get cut."

"Disabled. Where?"

And it went on like that until Fred, "The Working Man," arrived with the check and Vernon bought everyone forties and smokes and did his second-week-of-the-month dance out front. "Just call me the bird," he'd say, boogying barefoot into the night.

We were middle-class West Omaha boys out of our element, and we seemed to fit in just fine. Me, with my long, wavy home-permed hair and skate rags. T., with his crappy Toyota Celica with a hole in the muffler, hat cocked sideways with attitude. C., scoping things out, quiet as usual with his white t-shirt—built as we say here, like a brick shithouse.

School would start soon, and we'd have to wait until the weekends to come back. We always went back, and we always stayed too long. This was our little secret. Starting in our junior year, we went downtown, sporadically, to get most anything we desired. We were aware of pain and suffering, and we didn't have it any worse than the next guy. We were well fed and watered. Our families, all dysfunctional in their own ways, were concerned about our well-being. We had rules, curfews and, for the most part, we followed them. We came home when we were told. If we didn't, we were held accountable for our actions. We had things to accomplish. Things to become. We knew that. We also knew we liked to get bent. Why was it we were so desirous to singe our brains?

Fitting in and becoming that romantic renegade who didn't *seem* to care was important to me, then. Truth is, you hang around a place like Vernon's, and the weight of its sorrow, its disillusionment, starts to stick with you.

One night, heading back to Millard from downtown Omaha, C. drove his Trans Am madly. I was looking out the passenger window, trying not to pay attention, counting mile markers, wishing I was home. I was tired of the charade. I wanted out. But I also kept tagging along. He laughed and looked at me bizarrely. He said, "We could drive off this interstate right now! You want to?!" He swerved his car intentionally towards the shoulder.

"No fucking way man. I have stuff I want to do with my life!" I hollered back. We spent the next ten minutes in utter silence. There was something brewing inside of C. that I didn't want to be a part of anymore.

I wake up some nights, in a panic, that we are on that same stretch of the interstate. I think, quite possibly, he would have intentionally driven that car off the road if I would have gone along with it. Darkness wasn't alien. We didn't have to travel to find it. That night it was sitting right next to me, driving the car.

* * *

One Friday afternoon, we did our usual half-hour commute after school to Vernon's. We opened his front door and walked in after he didn't answer to find him dead on his couch. He had on what looked to be his only dark blue dress pants, no socks, and black, somewhat polished, half-tied shoes. He wasn't wearing a shirt. He was on the couch, flat on his back with his hands folded over his heart. "Hey, Vernon, wake up!" someone yelled. He didn't move. The three of us stood over him. His chest glistened with sweat. He smelled like vodka and BO. Someone checked his pulse. "Boo! I gotcha! You thought I was dead, didn't you."

"We hoped," T. said.

"Had to go to a job interview today. Look sharp, don't I?" he proclaimed, rising from the dead.

* * *

One night I was drinking my pack of Bartles and James wine coolers, and a kid, maybe twelve or thirteen, came upstairs and walked straight into Vernon's place without knocking. The little shitbird took two of my four wine coolers. He looked at me and said, "Whatta going to do about it?" Vernon told him to get on back downstairs and, "Tell your Daddy I ain't got nothing for him tonight."

* * *

Vernon had a few 45s. The one he played over and over was Pink Floyd's The Wall. When he got really drunk and didn't wander off, he'd start slur-singing, "We don't need no education…bom, bom, bom…We don't need no thoughts controlled, bom, bom-bom, bom. The darkside has a shady lady…Teacher leave these kids alone."

* * *

Senior send off. We went to Vernon's for one last hoorah. We told each other we weren't coming back. Why finally then, I'll never know. We spent two years driving back and forth to a part of the city that let us escape the middle-class confines of our lives and pretend we were free until we realized no running could change the men we were so desperately trying to become. T.'s girlfriend was pregnant. C. was heading to the Gulf War. I was contemplating college. *One last hoorah! Reflecting on our short and heavy lives.* It didn't take too long for T. to hug the toilet. His baseball cap had fallen off somewhere. He had some serious things ahead of him—a baby, possibly marriage. He was truly in love with his girlfriend, who was in love with him, too. He'd graduate high school, and he'd go on to be successful. The guy could work. Two of our friends had already dropped out of high school and were working full time—a thing that seemed enticing two years before, but now a daily 8-hour shift and responsibility seemed way out of my league.

Every time I reminisce and re-tell the climactic ending of that night, I tell the story this way… Florence Boulevard is where we used to go buy beer back in high school. Used to go to the corner liquor store until Vernon got smart and made us pick him up at his apartment instead. If we were going to be regulars he wouldn't have to stand out at the corner *no more*. All he ever wanted was his fifth of Skol. His apartment, with its light blue walls, smelled like a sweaty ass. There was no art on the walls, just his daughter's honor roll certificates and a turntable in the corner where he spun 45s. We ate gizzards there. We sang. We even danced with Vernon's wife until she started talking dirty to us. And the night she asked C. to feel her up and he didn't. The night she stabbed Vernon in the stomach because he couldn't get it up. That was the last time we bought beer on Florence Boulevard.

Never Talk to Strangers
12 Years in Prisons and
What Criminals Teach Me

1984 Serial Killer "The Nebraska Boy Snatcher" John Joubert Arrested

During the 1980s, twenty-year-old John Joubert was convicted of the murders of two boys in Nebraska. He'd gotten his start in Maine at the age of thirteen when he'd stab other children with pencils, razors, and other implements and found that he enjoyed hurting others. He tried strangling a boy and then when he was 18, he killed an eleven-year-old. Then he fled the town. From a broken home, Joubert had been an angry child, and he discovered both solace and power in striking out at others and getting away with it. In Nebraska, he looked for victims while volunteering in a Boy Scout troop. For him, the torture and murder of young boys was a way to relieve sexual tension. But as with all predators, the experience did not ultimately satisfy, so he would soon plan another.
—Katherine Ramsland, *Crime Library*

Where I come from—urban middle-America with apartment buildings, rows of split-level houses, manicured lawns and shopping malls, *Never talk to strangers* were four words constantly drilled into me and my friends because a lot of us were latchkey kids. We liked to believe the neighbors looked out for us.

When the serial killer John Joubert volunteered as a Boy Scout troop leader to lure and torture young boys, eventually kidnapping and killing two kids in the same part of Omaha where I lived—he became the nightmare, proof of the validity of those four words. None of us will forget the police crime sketch on milk cartons and plastered to street poles—this gruesome profile of a man with his mirrored sunglasses and hoodie pulled tight around his head. It was my neighborhood he did this in, and we wanted it back.

To sleep, most nights I curled up in a fetal position and stared at my bedroom window shades. It didn't matter what our parents said to console us, they were full of hate that this could happen in the Midwest, in the Heartland. So, we all re-invented worry, never again would talk to strangers because every one of them was him. We looked over our shoulders and learned to run the second an unfamiliar car stopped and someone inside asked for direction. It was the paranoia of the eighties in Omaha.

Around that same time, I fell at the bus stop, and stabbed an icicle into my knee. The school bus driver hollered, "Either board or I'm leaving." He left, and blood oozed as I limped back to the strip mall next to Country Club Village, the apartments where we lived. A guy came out of an office to help, tried to reach my folks at work without luck and then took me to school.

Mr. Shiver practically yanked my arm out of the socket for catching a ride from a complete stranger. "Someone you didn't even goddamn know!" That's when I knew my world had changed. These were the warzones of my home, which made us aware of our surroundings after peace and love had fallen on the cusp of cocaine—and everyone began living faster and meaner. This was when you, John, were living with your nightmares, perhaps calculating rapes, cuttings and killings. Ashes, ashes, John. No. No. No.

1990 The Murder of Christina O'Day

Christina had been babysitting overnight. Chris Garza and another perpetrator cut the phone line, broke in a basement window, tied her up, slit her wrists, took turns raping her, and then left her to die. For a few days after it happened, the police couldn't find him— his headshot on re-run on the news—the high school, the whole city of Omaha in an uproar. It was surreal, but it was our reality. In our high school hallways, I remember some of the friends Chris used to hang with (before he dropped out) saying they knew where he was hiding. The gossip. The uneducated comments from some of those people in a class of over 450 was beyond disturbing and immature. The child Christina was babysitting is still alive. The whole episode was replayed in the news—twenty six years later. Joe Chiodo of WOWT wrote:

> Christopher Garza has been resentenced for the 1990 murder of Christina O'Day. He was given 96 to 110 years in prison. Judge Polk said by factoring in the

"Good Time Law" and time already served, Garza would be eligible for parole in about 23 years. Garza is one of two men who beat, raped and murdered Christina O'Day as she was babysitting. At the age of 8, Beth Ann listened as the brutal crime unfolded.

Twenty-six years after the murder, a Supreme Court decision means one of O'Day's killers, then 16-year-old Christopher Garza, is in line for re-sentencing. That's based on new research showing at that age, a portion of a juvenile's brain is not fully developed.

WOWT 6 News spoke exclusively with Christina's mother, Sheila O'Day, following the sentencing. "It's been hard to come to terms over the years–the anger, frustration, sorrow–but it's time to move on. I feel justice has been served," she said.

"I wish I knew her. It's like your child left 26 years ago and you never saw them again. I believe she's at peace, but I still don't know her. I wish I could, I wish I could," Sheila O'Day told WOWT.

Beth Ann, now 34, returned from Georgia to attend the sentencing. She said it's a second chance at justice for O'Day.[1]

When I think of this murder from my adolescence, and of the safe split-level suburbia I came from, the fear is still ingrained in me. This is reality. Is there a killer inside me? If I think of my loved ones, and what I'd do if something like that happened to them, it scares me. We could talk about eye for an eye. We could talk about the death penalty. However, that's being extremely irrational and paranoid. What I know is that most prisoners aren't heinous animals—they aren't wicked criminals.

Wicked

In the article, "The effect of prison education programs on recidivism," in the *Journal of Correctional Education*, writer John Esperian notes: "Undoubtedly, some individuals—murderers, rapists, child molesters—are either unwilling or unable to live and work as honest, hard-working brokers within the framework of society. These dangerous anti-social cases need to be kept in confinement permanently for the safety of the community."

The Esperian article goes on to say:

As Jeffrey Rosen and Stephen Richards point out, however, in "Beyond Bars," more than 600,000 men and women are released from prison each year. The significance of these numbers is compounded by the fact that the US represents 5% of the world's population and nearly 25% of the world's prison population. Common sense would suggest that it is in society's best interest to do whatever it can to prepare released felons to function successfully in the outside world.

Fortunately, the numbers of those beyond rehabilitation are comparatively small, and most criminals, there is reason to believe, can turn from crime and live a productive, law-abiding life. Unfortunately, there is no litmus test to determine which individuals have the potential to change or to recidivate. And that, it would seem, is the primary reason that the opportunity must be extended to all incarcerated felons. For, as the research suggests, an education is the cornerstone to a structured life of work and learning--for former felons especially. "In a country," writes Vivian Nixon, "where second chances and opportunity are professed values, democratic access to high-quality higher education must include access for people in prison. We cannot bar the most vulnerable people from the very thing that has the greatest potential to change their lives."[2]

My First Metal Detector

Through the metal detector and after the pat-down by police, we find our seats on hard pews in the courtroom. We are here to bail out a "friend" who was drunk and beat up an innocent bystander—someone who probably looked at him wrong. I feel ashamed when I see him handcuffed, shirt torn from his Friday night brawl. I am not surprised, though. I'm disgusted that I am forking over money for bond. But I'm still in high school. I'm ignorant, and I don't think for myself. This is soon after Christina's death, and I am realizing, coming to understand that, in fact, the people I know could be criminals.

He stands silently as they read his indictment. Twice, he looks over at us, his few friends, like a pathetic dog. Just as quickly, they take him back into a jail cell. The judge continues to read off names of the accused. We cannot leave until he is done. A 60-year-old man hobbling on a cane is next. The front of his shirt brown with dried blood—accused of child molestation. I want to throw up, but I can't, and I can't leave.

It's over twenty years later, and I'm in my daughter's room. I have learned to think for myself—to do unto others as I'd want done to me. I'll never forget that courtroom scene, seeing that man with his stained and ripped t-shirt. As I tuck her into bed tonight I wonder: will monsters with canes and bloody shirts interrupt what should be precious thoughts of this world we live in? I cannot follow her everywhere. I can only teach her what to look out for, to repeat over and over, never to trust strangers.

Running with Wine

This is what I remember: and I wish you would go away. Walking down 60th Street with Chad, smoking Camels, going nowhere. I remember you passing us on the sidewalk, darting across the street toward Elmwood Park between dimly lit street lights—your shadow, running. And then screech! Brakes. Thud. Bottle breaking. Exhaust. You lying motionless on the street—tires spinning away. One of us ran to call for help. Both of us standing over you soon enough, checking your pulse again, staring at your face—beautiful, pale. Sirens ringing. Cops showing up. One of us pointing out the broken wine bottle you'd been carrying. The police officer kneeling down to inspect the bag the bottle was in. "It's corked. I believe she had plans for this evening."

1991 Hannibal Lecter

When I went to college, I became a Criminal Justice Major. My roommate was one, too. He and I had gone to the same high school together. Coincidence? In 1992 the psychological thriller *Silence of the Lambs* would win the Big Five Academy Awards for producing, directing, acting and screenwriting. I was grossly fascinated as to why criminals did what they did. The movie is a fictional portrayal—an amalgamation of serial killers. All criminals I imagined were comparable to Hannibal Lecter, to the delinquent in high school who raped and killed my friend. A friend I wouldn't be going dancing with again. A friend whom I could never call upon again for advice.

1994 O.J.

We interrupt the NBA finals to bring you this LIVE special report…Low speed pursuit—OJ—White Bronco…*Bloody Glove— Brentwood—Dream Team—Marcia Clark—Christopher Darden—Mark*

Fuhrman—Free O.J.—Nicole Brown Simpson—Ron Goldman—history of abuse—Fry O.J. … 95 Million Viewers glued to televisions across America as the bartender yells, "OJ and anything for a buck!"

1998

It's not just a criminal and a victim who are affected by crime. It goes much deeper than that. It affects whole families and communities. When she was nine years old and her father was sent away to prison for manufacturing and distributing methamphetamine, my cousin said she walked around with a target on her back for the next nine years she was in school—until graduation. Kids couldn't play with her. She was branded—was considered an outcast. "I was the bad influence."

2008 My First Finger-printing

I was in my office in the Midwest ten years ago. I was a new assistant professor with editing and publishing credentials. I was blazing new trails at the college, and the SOE (Supervisor of Education) from the federal prison in town was standing in the doorway of my office explaining a new writing program, an interagency agreement with the National Endowment for the Arts. One of the main objectives of the new program was a book of creative writing and art from inmates. I had been publishing books at small presses since I was an undergraduate. I knew the ins and outs of publishing but, more importantly, I knew how to teach complete strangers how to write. I had degrees on the wall that said so. And very quickly after my initial meeting and an extensive federal background check, I was at a federal prison getting my fingerprints stamped on official documents and my photo taken for my contractor's badge. I was given a drug urinalysis and was trained on procedure and protocol.

This is a minimum security prison. "No guards are present with me in the classroom? What if a student is disruptive?" I asked. "What if I think that my life is in danger?"

"We don't call them guards; we refer to them as correctional officers."

Whatever, I thought. When I'd told friends I was doing this work, I'd been gratified by their reactions. It had made me feel exotic, adventurous. It sounded cool to tell everyone I knew I was working in a prison, but honestly, I was scared. I had a very rigid belief of who all criminals were. I didn't understand the minimum security environment I was walking into. I hadn't tried to comprehend the word *rehabilitation,* and I had no idea about the huge monster our criminal justice system had morphed into. I was told there was a phone in the hall where I could call control for assistance or ask any of the staff on the floor for help. Right away, I was informed that these men were mostly non-violent offenders or white collar criminals. Or that they had trickled down through the system to this minimum security unit because of good time. No molesters. No murderers. No monsters. "Not that I know of," said the Supervisor of Education.

I would often bring in reading material for the men. One day that first year, I brought a month-old magazine. I showed it to the SOE who approved it and filled out the necessary paperwork. I took the magazine to the prison library, got it stamped **EDUCATION**, but forgot one last step. A student in class said to me, "You might want to black your address out. Most of us are good people here, but you just never know."

I was intimidated at first, like anyone would be. Media accounts are often negative portrayals of our criminal justice system, sensationalized propaganda to instill fear and promote, still after all these years, a tough-on-crime attitude. At first, I was afraid to use the same drinking fountain the men did. Paranoia. Did I think I would catch a disease? I was afraid to bend over at the drinking fountain, to take my eyes off anyone who might be behind me. I didn't have any idea, really, what world I was walking into. When a local asked me, "Why in the hell would you want to help prisoners? Seems like a waste of *my* tax money. Lock 'em up, forget about it," I didn't have a comeback. I knew, like any school teacher knows, the importance of education, but I had no idea how to effectively articulate what I was doing. I didn't have all my facts back then.

I am a guy who still walks both sides of this fence. I don't feel comfortable helping men who have premeditated and executed heinous crimes—3.3% of inmates in the federal system commit these atrocious acts of homicide, aggravated assault, and kidnapping offenses.[3]

2009 Welcome to San Quentin

When I first brought the news home that I'd be working in a prison, my wife was concerned, but she listened. The pay was good and, like most young couples, we needed the money. I reassured her everything was going to be fine. Part of our contractor training through the National Endowment for the Arts entailed working with the William James Association where we would visit some California state prisons and study their arts in corrections programs. So in my second year, as I filled out waivers about my safety—"The CDCR

will not negotiate for you in a hostage situation" —concerning my
trip to San Quentin, I was scared. But I was already invested. There
are lines we cross all the time in our lives, purposefully and with
good intentions. There are lines we know never to cross. This was
the dilemma.

Stage fright doesn't exist. Say yes when the Arts ask you to leave
your daughters at home and read for and work with the hardest
of men. "The correction officers will not negotiate for you in a
hostage situation." Hear and understand this. This isn't a game. Read
the contract—black and white. Think urinal gassings, homemade
shanks, newspaper daggers. Pack your funeral shoes and black boots.
YouTube San Quentin and bypass Johnny Cash. "You are a skinny
little white man," a colleague says. "They won't leave you unattended."
This trip is nonrefundable. You understand?

"Don't forget your lube!" the town cop says.

> <u>DO NOT WEAR DENIM OR BLUE TO THE FACILITY</u>.
> Never allow yourself to be without staff or security. The DOC does
> not tolerate sexual harassment—notify authorities immediately. Do
> not engage in personal transactions with any inmate. Do not discuss
> personal affairs—confine yourself to teaching art. Our program
> depends on a narrow and conservative view of our role in the facility.
> It is a felony for anyone to assist in an inmate's escape. Bringing
> guns, weapons of any kind is prohibited—this includes tear gas,
> explosives, and also cocaine, liquor or any other narcotics.

"They will try you, immediately. They will see how far they can
push, how much you will let on, how much you will provide. Believe
me. I see it every day," a Correctional Officer says.

Hop off Sir Frances Drake Boulevard, and just like that, you're
in their world. "Prime estate in San Fran," the driver says. Pass
through the first armed and guarded entrance after they check the
trunk into 432 acres that house California's only gas chamber and
death row for condemned inmates. Park the car in the neighborhood
where staff and their families live (some in trailers they pull behind
their pickups because it's too expensive to live anywhere else).

When a prisoner picks you up in a state vehicle, drives you to
the Sally Port, act like it's all natural. Watch him patiently change
the dial of the radio. There you will show ID and be invisibly
hand-stamped as you are received through three separated
and locked iron-gate corridors. Hear a man tell you about the
problems prisoners face with parole boards, the Governor's
inevitable final say. Hear him laugh, kind of, tell you how this

place, demographically, is compared to the country of China. "China." Hear the echo. "China—a country—get that, man! We get the newspaper here. Get a lot of things you probably don't want to know about. State made chicken coops bigger, on account they weren't humane for a chicken. Made them cages bigger. We petitioned. Did the math. Proved our holes aren't large enough for a Labrador Retriever. Shit, I suppose I shouldn't complain—360 guys sleeping in my room—the gymnasium. Believe that. I can show you, you want."

"Who's house is this? Our House!" Fear the Mexican Mafia over the three-story barbed and fenced courtyard doing their hour-long session of strenuous organized calisthenics. See their shadows—push-ups, deep-knee bends. "Hoo! Hoo! Hoo! Hoo!" You are outside with the pigeons but locked in. There is a memorial garden for slain officers to your left and a chapel to your right. Walk through the courtyard and keep your eyes on. The convicted men are in blues and t-shirts. "Fresh Fish. Fresh Fish!" A line of new prisoners in their fluorescent orange jumpsuits single file—heads slumped—eyes zig-zagging. "Fresh Fish!"

Arrive at the entrance of the Prison Arts Program. "My name is Bird Man. Bird Man," an old gray man says. "Birds like me. Land right on my shoulder."

"It's the truth," another inmate says.

"Of course it is. Of course it is. Why he lie about birds. You see it, right here." Walk with your group inside. An inmate immediately approaches you. "You ever have that dream, the one where you have to choose your ears or your eyes? Which one would you pick? Here," he says, "we try to forget both."

2011 What Critics Say

Critic David Doody reviewed some of my first poems in *The American Poetry Journal*, poems about visiting San Quentin and my childhood. He wrote: "Such experiences make it hard to know why someone would place himself among the people who have been convicted of crimes like the one that took place in Reese's childhood neighborhood and have left him with a gnawing fear for his daughters' well-being…Caught in the enigma of how humans can both love and hurt, Reese is torn between his constant drive to protect his daughters ('You want to ride your bike around the block-/by yourself') and his desire to help the sort of people whose actions have made the world a dangerous place in which his daughters need protecting."[4]

Why is it that when strangers rather than loved ones start to question our intentions and well-being we listen more? This is a question I ask inmates often, but seldom ask myself. Besides thoughtful reviews of my work, I have also had the great fortune to work with some gifted writers. Here, award-winning author Kent Meyers points out some very important things: "In entering the prison, you enter the most alien of all possible cultures and communities. And what do you find? People—people pretty much like yourself or your students, or even maybe your daughters. But— and this is so great as an idea if not as a fact of human nature— what you also discover is that the people outside the prison *could* be inside, and some of them maybe should be, or at least that the prisoners who seem so alien turn out to have come from families and communities and schools just like those you knew and know."

We as humans are indecisive and unpredictable. We are of two minds, and when we fear or are uncertain, we throw up walls. Is life merely a riddle of walls—prisons of our own making? Part of my journey, the things that have influenced me, are crimes and criminal activity. I never wanted to admit it. But if I look deep, it's always been there.

Prison Pruno

I stand in the Sally Port—this old-fashioned and small gateway in and out of the prison. I notice one of many signs hanging on the old stone walls. *Don't forget to buy your San Quentin T-Shirt—TODAY ONLY.* I remember my colleague insisting, "Bring me back a souvenir, and don't be cheap about it."

I'm standing in the parking lot overlooking the San Francisco Bay, inhaling its salty shell breeze. This 432 acres is the most desired waterfront property; experts believe developers would pay $2 billion.

I approach the C.O.—the T-shirt vendor—and like everything here, it's surreal. There is a line. There are hoodies, various apparel— all for sale. Proceeds to help sustain San Quentin's Honor Guard Program. I buy two identical t-shirts that replicate a Jack Daniels bottle and read:

> **San Quentin Prison**
> **Penn No. 1**
> **1852**
> **Cell-brewed**
> **Pruno**

"So," I say to the C.O., "you're selling t-shirts that promote a crime within the prison to raise money for the Honor Guard?"

"Yeah."

"Fair enough," I respond, as I turn and enter a vehicle driven by an inmate who will escort us off grounds. I flash him the t-shirt and ask him if he wants one. "No way, man!" he says in disgust and a bit surprised. "I'm living this hell."

Brand

Fifteen out of twenty-two guys in the class are inked. Blue-black brands, their inimitable statements. One student's forearm is a mess of calligraphy, and when I lean down to read his arm horizontally it says *LIFE*—when he turns his arm upside down, *DEATH*. "Interesting," I say out loud, and it is. Someone put a lot of thought into that. I ask the other students in class to write down their tattoos on a piece of paper, or show me if they prefer. One asks, "Do you have a tattoo, Dr. Reese?" And I put my leg up on the desk and pull up my pant leg, push down my black sock. *GONZO*.

"What does that say? Gonzo? What's that supposed to mean?"

"It means immersing yourself in the story. Instead of writing about someone getting a tattoo, you go get one yourself and tell everyone how it feels to be permanently marked."

Body art is a statement, a mark of authority. *M.O.B. Money Over Bitches; Loose Lips Sink Ships; What Is, Will Be; Loyalty: Born 2 Fail; Destined 2 Succeed; Death B4 Dishonor; Virgin Mary; Jesus Christ; Heart; Rose; Wild Wild 100's; Suckafree; Mister Smooth.* And on the eyelids of one man there are two tattoos that read—*GAME OVER*.

In here, as I watch men peel off layers of themselves—stripped of freedom, some trying to find redemption, I still question them. "Who the hell has the tattoo—Fuck the ATF DEA US Marshals—?" And I see X put down his head, his face turns red. He slowly raises his hand, kinda grins.

"I seen it," another classmate of his says. "It's on his back."

Immediately I flash back to high school, in some cramped apartment drinking a forty with god knows who, when I see some Nazi punk with *SKINS* tattooed across his forehead backwards. I tell the class the story. How we all hated the kid but didn't know what to do. They laugh. Cuss under their breath. Shake their heads. X is deadpan, looking out the iron window.

Hoses

One day in prison, a student in class told me a story about one of his greatest regrets. What I began to discover was that addiction, in all of its gross immaturity, will make people go to extreme measures. The student, an inmate in his late twenties, was built, as we say here on the plains, like a brick shithouse. He and I talked briefly at the back of the class. "My grandfather had a Farmall 300.

You had a need for hoses for your tractor so you could raise the lift cylinders and tilt bucket with the hydraulics. When the hose was missing—I'm sure he was shocked. When he asked me if I'd seen it, I lied. He said, 'I've had that tractor, I don't know how long. No one's ever taken a hose off it.' What he didn't know was that I used the hose to cook meth. I can't keep feeling guilty about my past. I'm done paying that bill. But I tell you, I wish I'd never took that hose."

Voice

I am grading freshman essays at the private Catholic college where I work. Too many papers about exhaustive road trips without hitchhikers. Anorexia. The death penalty. Abortions. One about the Future Farmers of America. You don't have to grow up in the country to be a member. I never knew that. Most essays about families say they are dysfunctional. They always are. But sometimes it still scares me what students reveal. Like when Carlos writes, *That night, when my father pointed his hunting rifle at my head and said he was going to put a bullet between my eyes, I knew I had to say something. That's the first time I used my voice to make a difference.*

The phone in my office rings and it's Willow. "Dad," she says, her voice shaky and exhilarated. "Can I get my ears pierced?" At that moment, she could have asked for a pony and I'd have probably given it to her. How exciting it is to hear a child's anticipation. The delight, instead of darkness.

GED Test Result Day

"Hey, I passed—I really did it!" Two inmate students high five each other. "Way to go man! I knew you could do it." The one pats the other on the back. Men happy to be graduating. Their smiles frozen on Polaroid—ear to ear to sky, soaring alone now. Free.

"GED test result day is always fun around here," the Supervisor of Education says.

New Folsom Prison

There are few words for *razor on flesh*. For *scream. Black. Blue. Cut. Wet.* I see some of you bandaged at the wrist or forearm. Bandaged at the belly and throat. You are cutting to get out.

Entertainment

I'm with C.J. Box, Craig Johnson, and some other award-winning commercial crime writers, all of us representing a genre as keynote speakers. I'm reading poetry about prisoners—the hard truths of coming to terms with why people are incarcerated. The MC of the grand event, in the historic ballroom packed with hundreds of people paying banquet prices for a good cause, stands up to retrieve the microphone when I have finished a poem—she wants to stop my presentation short. I can see in her expression that my presentation isn't commercial enough. I don't hand the mic to her. Instead, I read another poem about the war on drugs, this war on race, this war on humanity. When I finish my ten-minute presentation, I hand the microphone to the MC who looks her part here in the west—a shiny and stiff cowboy hat—everything amazingly gunslinger cliché.

"Well, that was depressing," she mutters to me while simultaneously covering the microphone. She smiles and then turns back to the crowd to tell another joke.

A few years later, I am in the same historic town, presenting again. I make a point to go and listen to a recent Edgar Award-winning author. His details and description are very good. I am captivated by his honesty and what he says about crime—that he doesn't know a lot about it. After his presentation, I see him walking in the casino, riding a high after the day's events. I introduce myself, tell him I enjoyed his reading and talk on craft. "Oh, I totally have to pick your brain to find out what criminals are really like," he says to me. That is the third time a famous crime writer has said that to me.

2014 The Track

I'm walking the prison yard when an inmate student next to me begins to tell me a story I've never forgotten. "You know, one of the prisons they had me at, I could step into a corner of my cell and get a sliver of sunlight—it would hit me right here." He cranes his neck, closes his eyes and traces a line down the side of his cheek and over a hard vein in his neck. "Right here for about a half an hour. That was the only sunlight I'd see. It's mental deprivation. It works.

"Hell, most guards don't know what you're in for. They don't care. We were loaded on a 747 one winter, and we were standing on the tarmac without any jackets—bunch of us. Just a t-shirt and orange pants, no socks, no shoes. They had our legs chained at the ankles so tight I was bleeding all over my feet—freezing. Scars are still here." He stops, puts his leg on a bench and pulls down his sock to show me.

"See these flowers," he says. "They're closed at night, and in the morning they open. Stay like that most of the day. I don't know what they're called. I had the same ones by my front steps. The stems feel plastic, almost fake. They break easily. We aren't supposed to touch them here.

"You know, I'm no killer or sicko. My whole stint that got me here lasted only five months. Meth will eat you up. Fifteen years I'll be down for an addiction I couldn't shake. Could have never imagined. When my daughter used to come visit me, I'd be behind those glass partitions. She'd tell me, 'Daddy, roll down this window.' I'd say, 'I can't, Honey.' She'd ask, 'When you gonna come home?' 'Soon', I'd tell her. Now she wants to know the date. She'll be graduated by then."

For eleven years I've walked this blacktop, a quarter-mile track, with my students at this prison camp. They are an eclectic mix of criminals, men with PhDs and GEDs. I ask them to write down five things they've never noticed. Sometimes a student will say, "It's just the same old, same old. It's prison. Nothing's changing in here."

Today in front of one of the housing units, the one with no AC, I see a miniature banana tree. It isn't blooming, but all the same, it's a bit out of place here in the Midwest. "Enjoy it while you can," one inmate in the horticulture program says. "This is its last year."

Forbes magazine rated this prison camp one of "America's 10 Cushiest Prisons" in 2009. In describing the facility, Asher Hawkins wrote, "The winters are tough, and the nearest city of any size is at least an hour away, but this is a stand-alone minimum-security facility with a staff that's not too tough on prisoners. White-collar cons can take classes in accounting, business administration and business management."[5] I wonder how much time Asher Hawkins spent at the prison camp. I cannot speak as an authority of the Federal Bureau of Prisons, nor am I speaking on their behalf—but, this is what I've learned.

I just visited Washington, DC this past summer. Over two million visitors pass through the Smithsonian Castle on the National Mall, where they have their exhibition gardens. Maybe you have been there. This prison camp with its gothic style structure reminds me a lot of the gardens there; it's that nice. The lawn here is perfectly mowed and trimmed, petunias and perennials aligned in an array of designs and a kaleidoscope of color. On a busy day there might be twenty-five pruners, and ten other men keeping the twenty-four acres mowed. Private wells owned by the Federal Bureau of Prisons keep the grass lush and greener than the surrounding neighborhood lawns. Family homes which surround this prison went up in value. In fact, this may be the only place in the nation where a public street runs through a federal prison. There's no barbed wire here, just a three-foot cast-iron fence. The current population of the camp is 479 with a maximum capacity of 850. I've been here when it has exceeded capacity. New laws and a reduction of mandatory minimums has cleared room.

This black track is smooth. One of my former students added up the miles he had walked over the past few years, "Enough to cross the country—twice." Barbed wire or not, how men spend productive time in prison is a concern. One in every three people of working age has some sort of criminal record.[6] That's over 100 million Americans by my calculations. Chances are really, really good you know someone who has been to jail or prison.

One of my students and I are walking quietly. I want to ask him something but hesitate. I've kicked myself later for not speaking up when I have a question, so I ask, "How many men do you think walk this path and contemplate really changing their lives for the better?" And I continue, "I walk around here and listen, and can almost guarantee that some of these men will be back by the way they are talking to each other."

"It's where I come to clear my head," he says, "to get some peace. I know what you mean." In a recent issue of our prison literary journal, we published a piece by a father and son who are currently incarcerated together. The father is very upset with the way the criminal justice system has treated him because he is a non-violent offender. I agree with him. There are probably other alternatives. However, men who are guilty and are incarcerated need to own their mistakes. The copy editor of the journal and I were talking about this particular piece before we were ready to publish it, and she said, "He might be 'defending himself' against the hurt and loss that family members might (rightly?) be upset with him for.... I'm sure all the difficulties he mentions are real—but who caused them?"

The copy editor is a nun, a person who has devoted her life to helping others. She's an excellent editor and writer. She taught Scripture for decades and published the book *Beginning Biblical Studies* and some biblical commentary for laypeople. As we continued to edit the piece via email, she remarked: "It distresses me that Sessions says he wants to return to the longest sentence possible. If no one asks, *What was leading this person to taking/making/selling drugs?* (or other criminal activity), there will be no viable alternatives to that *Throw 'em in jail and throw away the key approach.* Some rehab programs work— but the *catch* is always that the offender needs to choose it and work at it. *It's somebody else's fault* surely stands in the way of such a choice."

As I've grown out of my rebellious and disillusioned thirties, I have less tolerance and empathy for people who refuse to acknowledge their faults and do something about them. My next-door neighbor said he was tired of hearing people complain. He said, "If you have a hard time breathing, quit smoking. If you can't see, open your eyes."

This Isn't Dress Rehearsal

It's 53 degrees this afternoon. Tomorrow, the clock will spring ahead. In five minutes the still obnoxiously loud grade-school bell will alarm the neighborhood. In line at the chain-link fence with some other fathers who have shown up, I'm waiting for you, my daughters. Today, recess should never end. In two months one of you will leave this place for middle school, the other ascend to second grade. Some things never change. I claw my hands into the chain-link that seems so much shorter now. I see the tire-swing, the basketball hoop without a net, blacktop and worn tetherball. I'm not old enough to wish I were back in your shoes, not with the math homework you're assigned. But, there's the aching for some of that freedom. Maybe that's why none of the fathers standing outside this fence say a word. When I shared the rough draft of this reflection in class, a prisoner said, "That's one fence I never minded being behind."

Girls, do you know how much I'm going to miss these days? This magical moment on all our faces when we see each other between these boundaries, waiting to go home?

Writing for Reentry

I'm not a liberal professor who is necessarily soft on crime. Public safety is still the number one concern. There is no definitive answer to fixing our criminal justice system, just like there is no decisive answer to fixing any problem. In the past forty-eight years, we were told there was one simple way to solve this "public enemy number one" problem—a lock-and-leave mentality. By simply barring someone in a cage for some diligent time, he or she would come out a better person. There is no single permanent fix for anything of this nature. I understand that not all people are locked up for drug related charges, but almost half of federal prisoners are in for drug crimes. There are some common sense solutions.

Two years ago, I was appointed to teach writing for reentry classes at the state men's and women's prisons in South Dakota—a much different setting than the "cushy" federal prison I've spent so much time in. At the state prisons, 57% of the inmates are non-violent offenders. 86% of women are non-violent—65% of whom are drug offenders (internal monthly report April 2018).

We cannot ignore our drug crisis. It is an emergency whether you want to call it an opioid, heroin, fentanyl or carfentanil (an elephant sedative) epidemic; these drugs are killing thousands. This is a national health emergency that needs to be addressed. Tough on crime will never fix this. It's an illness. I sent an email warning one of the unit managers at the state prison to be aware of these dangerous drugs. He wrote back, "Water-stained mail that comes into the prison now is immediately thrown out for fear that it could be laced with this stuff."

Back to the Track

I really like this student I'm talking to on the track. He's a lot more honest than most people I know outside of this prison. He means what he says. He's the kind of guy you want on your side. He's a good listener. He's in here for drugs, and honestly, I don't care. I'm not the judge and jury. We are beyond that. It's my job to help him never come back here. He's an amazing writer, spinning yarns of deep-woods Missouri kin. So it's surprising to me when he asks what specific tree is in front of us with bark peeling off the trunk.

"River Birch," I tell him.

"That's it. How did I forget that? You know before I got here I was at a different prison. Most of us trickle down the system to get to a place like this if we are lucky. And most prisons aren't like this. I never saw anything green. Just concrete, dirt, and razor-wire. I remember arriving here in a mini-van. The instant I got out I saw this tree. I walked right towards it and touched it. I grabbed a hold of it and squeezed. The guard said, 'get back here; I need to process you!' I told him, just hold on a second. I haven't seen a tree in three years. And I wrapped my hands around its trunk. Squeezed so tight. I'm a country boy. To be denied the outdoors was like a death sentence for me."

I'm walking the yard. I'm thinking sunshine, handcuffs, plexiglas, scars.

FLASHBACK, 2016

It's in the news again. I email my father to see if he remembers. He emails back, "Garza doesn't look like he feels sorry for what he did. I'm not reading anything about rehabilitation or remorse." I agree. By now, Garza's brain has had a chance to fully develop. He's had plenty of time to own his heinous sins. Social media, the newspaper and television accounts are alive. All of a sudden, these fears and this indescribable sickness in my gut emerges. In the *Omaha World Herald* Erin Grace writes:

> The commotion woke up Beth Ann, who then endured three hours of frozen fear until she heard someone leave around 5:30 a.m. She then drifted off

to sleep and woke again when Chris's alarm clock went off at 6:30 a.m. Beth Ann slipped on some pants, crept outside her bedroom and peered inside her mother's room, where she saw blood on the pillowcases and sheets. Creeping downstairs, she saw Sunshine's feathers all over the floor and the home in disarray. She reached for the phone and dialed 911, but the line was dead. So Beth Ann opened the front door and ran to a neighbor's house. "I rang the doorbell five times, but nobody answered," she testified in 1990. "I went to the next house and rang the bell three times, but nobody came. I went to the third house and rang it once, and they were home. When he answered the door, I told him, 'I think my baby sitter's dead.'"[7]

A lot of us at Millard South were shaken by this crime. To say we had school spirit would be awkward. I'm not sure what we had left except a rock by the entrance of the school in memory of Christina's life.

Some of us moved after high school, putting distance between ourselves and our past. I made my way back for grad school in Omaha and was sitting at a bar having drinks with someone I vaguely knew from high school, an aspiring writer like myself. I asked her if she could write about it, if she ever had. "No. I tried. What can you say? That we fucking hate the guy for what he did. What good does that do? Doesn't bring her back. What about you?" she asked.

"I'm trying. Surely there's something I can write to make some sense of it all."

The newspaper said there were over 700 people at her funeral. We had to sit in some hall by the church and watch it all on a teleprompter. I got up at the end and walked past the stilled, zoned-out and tear-stained faces of my classmates. I looked across the parking lot at the sea of mourners. I spotted some of the guys Garza hung out with before he dropped out. They were trying to act cool, smoking their cigarettes, flicking the ashes, glancing up at the church and away again. They were smiling. One of them pinched his cigarette, took a drag and blew smoke rings. I knew they knew where Garza was hiding—this was before he turned himself in proclaiming his innocence. It makes me sick how disconnected people were, even then. She was brutally murdered, and they seemed to be worried about their image.

STATS

I wonder about intention versus attention. All the media's devotion paid to crime. The general public has this *It doesn't affect me* attitude when it comes to prisoners, when, in reality, most all of us are guilty of crime, petty or not. Some of us just never got caught. Check out the new movement, *We Are All Criminals*.

When asked the question, *Why should I care?* I can tell you, there are 1,800 state and federal correctional facilities and 3,200 local and county jails, according to Christopher Ingraham of the *Washington Post*. To put these figures in context, we have slightly more jails and prisons in the U.S.—5,000 plus—than we do degree-granting colleges and universities. In many parts of America, particularly the South, there are more people living in prisons than on college campuses.[8]

I work at two prisons within a fifty-mile-radius of my house. Both those prisons were colleges less than forty years ago. Each year we spend billions on criminal justice but spend less and less on education. Right now there are approximately 2.2 million Americans behind bars. Each year more than 600,000 inmates are released from federal and state prisons, and another 11.4 million individuals cycle through local jails. Around 70 million Americans have some sort of criminal record—almost one in three Americans of working age.[9] From 1980 to 2008, the number of people incarcerated in America quadrupled, from roughly 500,000 to 2.3 million people. Combining the number of people in prison and jail with those under parole or probation supervision, 1 in every 31 adults, or 3.2 percent of the population is under some form of correctional control.[10]

A recent 2013 RAND Corporation report found strong evidence that correctional education plays a role in reducing recidivism: "Education is key to turning our justice system around. The study concluded that every $1 spent on prison education translated into $4 of savings during the first three years, post-release."[11] If nothing else, if you are just worried about "Your Tax Dollar," that's why you should care. More importantly, though, is that prisoner education helps transform lives on both sides of the fence.

You can lock a person up and let them out after so long. Maybe during their incarceration you teach them a trade—that's great. What you also have to do is help them tap into the emotional instabilities that brought them to prison in the first place. If a person never comes to terms with himself or herself, you are just going to send an angry person right back out into society.

I was eating lunch with my friend Bob, a Philly transplant who has been a local in my city longer than I have been alive.

He's the former baseball coach at the college where I teach, the former interim dean of the college, a guy they named the new college baseball field after. He's a smart man and a good coach. He understands that life, just like baseball, is a game of failure more often than not. Most times you go to bat you aren't a success. I said, "I wish, after ten years, I still had a quick comeback for these people who always ask me why I do this work at the prisons." He didn't blink an eye and said, "If we all aren't trying to chip away at the iceberg, what's our alternative?"

A Student Speaks of Her Sister's Murder

At Mount Marty College a student is writing about her sister who was murdered. She doesn't know how to tell her story once she has written the brief introduction about the last time her sister and family were all home together for the holidays. The details of the interior of the house—the piano music and cheer—the warm, welcome feeling of family sings on the page. She is worried about the chronological order of things. She is also concerned that these details won't mean anything to the reader. When she finishes presenting her rough draft she continues to tell the story. She describes the random act of murder as it was told to her by authorities. She describes news accounts. Eventually, with my encouragement, she writes about it some more. The in-class dialogue this produces helps to some extent—although I don't think anyone fully heals from tragedy like this.

During workshop, the student said she never found out if the killer was mentally ill or why he did what he did. "Authorities gave him tests and concluded that he was..." (and the student can't think of the right words to say)—"that something was wrong with the man. They didn't know if he was on drugs at the time. He claimed he thought he was 100 miles away in Oakland, California, and he was stranded, and when he saw lights he walked towards them—towards the restaurant and bar her sister and friend had just left for the evening. When he demanded keys, they wouldn't give them to him. He chased them back to the restaurant and bar, back to the front door they were running to—but the door was locked. That's when he killed her. Later, the police found him five miles away with her car. It was a done deal. The cops had him, the stolen vehicle and the murder weapon."

She proceeded to talk about the trial. Before she went into the courtroom, she said, "We had a quick briefing with our lawyer. I asked him if we could expect to see some of the murderer's family. The lawyer said no one had come to visit him the entire time he had been locked up."

She gives us a play-by-play of the court proceedings, with tears running down her face. She said the man who killed her sister sat silent as stone. Eventually, her sister's friend who was with her that night, read her victim's statement.

"I didn't take my eyes off the guy in court," she said. "I sat in the middle of my parents with both my arms around them. He just sat there staring blankly ahead. Cold. Lifeless. He wouldn't look at me. My sister's friend read her speech. She painted a picture of my sister—of her life—of how adventuresome and how funny she was. Her statement captured my sister's sense of humor. And for a few seconds I saw the man that murdered my sister almost grin at the funny, loving and kind person that was being described. And then he must have remembered that he was the one on trial, the one that killed her. And his face again went blank."

BEING Evil VS. DOING Evil

At one of my co-editor, Sister Marielle Frigge's, presentations at the prison, we discussed "being evil" and "doing evil" in class. Later, when I emailed her about that classroom discussion, this is what she had to say:

> I think the discussion started with a student raising the question, noting that since he "got religion," some of his relatives were shunning or at least looking down on him somewhat. In the course of that, he suddenly asked, "Do you think there are people who are evil?" I said that I do believe that evil exists—not as a character with horns and a pitchfork, but as a power that can and sometimes does influence people.
>
> I mentioned the book, *People of the Lie* (subtitle: *Hope for Healing Human Evil*), by M. Scott Peck. Peck writes that his counseling experience convinced him beyond doubt that evil exists, and that he had witnessed it in action in several exorcisms. Then I referred to a clinical psychologist (she recommended the book to me—it was quite a few years ago), and she was the one who gave the example of people she had encountered in her practice who came to her "for help," yet seemed completely determined to act against any advice or guidance she would give. One of them had given a son a shotgun for a Christmas

present, knowing the boy was suicidal…

> …in light of Scripture and Catholic theology—no human being is "born evil," but is created in the image of God. The choices a person makes have a lot to do with whether one does "evil deeds," but of course, every human being's choices are limited to some degree by many, many factors—and that's where it gets messy.… Many people also don't make a distinction between BEING evil and DOING evil."

The man who started the discussion in class has since been transferred to a high-level facility for breaking the rules at the federal prison camp. During class, I considered him one of my best students, thought that he was on the straight and narrow, that he was a changed man. I thought he had made the turn. He asked the right questions. He motivated others in class to be better men. He had a lot of us fooled. When I think of him today, I am truly disappointed. So are his former classmates. He is a talented man. He had some writing chops. But he was still conning inside. What's he going to do when he is released if he never confronts his evil-doing? Most times when I think of him, I feel fooled for putting my faith in him. I feel a little naïve. And, I'm pissed off because he lied to me. I don't have empathy for people who lie right to my face. He knows the difference between doing evil and being evil. You want to believe as a school teacher that you can help everyone. But I've realized there are a few students I never will be able to connect with. I thought I had gotten to know him, but he proved to be stranger still.

Cat vs. Car

Recently, a student at the prison decided to stand up and interrupt his classmates because he wasn't happy about a typo—a mistake someone had made typing up one of his rough drafts (I have a few Mount Marty College students type up the prisoners' works for them and help them with some initial editing). He said, "It says *cat* here. It's supposed to say *car*. This changes everything." When I told him to sit down, that it was our mistake, that it was a typo that could be fixed and we could talk about it later, it made him furious. And by fault I also added, "You know, I've never had anyone type up work of mine—ever."

He glared at me and said, "I'm not even fucking listening to you now." That week he was sent to the SHU for anger issues.

Remorse

At a recent California Lawyers for the Arts in Corrections Conference in Los Angeles, I told the story about my friend's brutal murder when the subject of heinous people—good versus evil— was brought to the table. One of my colleagues asked, "Why do you think he did it?"

I'd heard that his father was in prison or had been locked up around the same time. Was that motivation? Did the lack of parental supervision play into murder? There was a rumor of drugs— although I didn't read any police reports that confirmed this. It's grotesque, considering his education. He was smart—I know at one point he got good grades. I asked him for help on my homework a couple of times in junior high. I can see him in our classroom. I want to reach out and shake him. Tell him, *Wake up, man! The path you are going down is all wrong.*

I want to drive to that house where Christina was babysitting and get those girls out of there. We all do. But it's too late. Why do we, her friends, and all those who loved and cared for her want to change things, and why doesn't he care? Why did he do it? I puzzle at this question, and recently asked it of a friend of mine, Joe Erickson, a police officer. "There are different kinds of criminals. Some simply do not learn, and continue to make mistakes. Some, however, feel they are above the law and are not able to feel things that most people can feel, like remorse."

I've spent the last year doing over a hundred hours of ride-alongs with Sergeant Javier Murgia in our small city. He was Officer of the Year in 2017—he was also a former student at the college where I teach. To truly understand crime and all of its repercussions I need to see it on the front end. Spending a night riding along with him isn't enough. I vowed to spend at least 200 hours acting as his shadow before I began to tell the bigger story. On slow nights I record a lot of interviews with him. I had to ask him what he believed a heinous criminal was.

"I believe the heinous criminals we hear about operate at a different level. It is difficult to really figure out what makes them tick. All humans are capable of and oftentimes do make mistakes. Most people recognize the errors they commit and show some form of remorse or regret. Then you have those that show no regret and have no remorse; there is an obvious disconnect going on there. Some believe it is mental illness while others prefer to say it is pure evil. I see it as something that cannot be ignored. It is as if the person does not know or has chosen to ignore the difference between right and wrong."

A Ladder, an Oar, a Walk-in-Closet at San Quentin

Training at San Quentin prison, I had access almost everywhere. Inside 4 1/2 ft. wide by 7 ft. high by 11 ft. long cells—the size of your typical walk-in closet. The kitchen where a man stood on a ladder stirring a cauldron full of spaghetti sauce with an oar. Medieval rooms, a 164-year-old cavern in the exercise-yard. Even condemned row, where a longtime C.O. said, "The men sentenced to die aren't animals. They've made some horrible decisions. Some premeditated."

At a cocktail party one evening, I met a man who taught yoga to men on Death Row. "They are human beings," he said. It was odd to hear this with a glass of red wine in my hand. It was different from the fear I feel, the anguish I still possess over my friend who was raped and killed, the tight knot in my heart that every parent has, the horrendous feeling of knowing if that happened to my child what I might do. Eye for an eye while the Pinot Noir stained my tongue. Uncertainty when the glass was empty.

2018

I was talking to my cousin—the one I mentioned earlier with a target on her back since age nine. She said, "I heard on the news this morning (while emailing you) that an older man charged with murders in LA, confessed to 90 other murders of women—some of which, maybe all, not sure, took place in Omaha in the 70s. Freaking crazy.

"It's all so interesting...disturbing. I must admit I am more afraid than I used to be as a woman. I am much more aware of my surroundings and take extra caution. I wish I didn't have to, but I can't pretend these terrible things aren't happening all over, and that they can't happen to me, because they can happen to anyone. I do hope that having some extra edge protects me. I am not naive to the reality of society. So far that has worked in my favor."

Jesus Christ Pose

In a theatre practicum in San Quentin, I watch you, a prisoner, standing in the center of the room. You raise your hands, palms up, head dangling down, your Jesus Christ pose. You begin to stand on one foot. The room is quiet. People begin shifting in their seats. Minutes pass. You begin to lose your balance. "Every morning," you say, "after my foster father left for work, she made me stand in the corner like this." And when your desperate left foot hits the ground, you scream in the voice of a child being beaten. Now I understand why some of you are here.

Silent and Still as Stone

After dinner-count, I see you on the stairwell gazing out the large turn-of-century windows, each pane a looking glass into that world where you once belonged. I never say hello to you.

You don't see me looking down these stairs at your back, your khaki shirt, your gray, receding hair. I climb the next flight, look out the window to see if I can decipher what it is you are fixed on—parking lot? Midday traffic? Over the fence are homes. Families racing about. A kid on a skateboard ollies over a manhole. Two speed-walkers point and chatter as they chase each other.

But shit, man, maybe I have it all wrong. I see the Chevys and Fords, hear the engines call, the glass-pack's throaty cough. Maybe we're more alike than I thought, waiting patiently, considering that getaway car.

Coda

I suppose it's just habit when I pass the guys in the yard and ask, "How's it going?" Always since I was a kid, I'd ask, "How's it going?" To strangers—to friends. Today, as I pass men in their prison-issued khakis and numbered shirts, one stops and tells me, "Don't you know—you're not supposed to ask us that?" And those few seconds that we stand face to face—I try to conjure up what I should have said before a C.O. orders him away. What I should have said was, "No, I didn't know." How stupid of me not to think of something smarter to say. Me, the teacher, who can leave this prison any time I like.

Things that have altered me are crimes. When I was young, I felt like an outsider, a stranger (especially as an only child), someone who was never afraid to ask, "Why?" I've never shaken that. Nor do I intend to. We as humans are indecisive—are unpredictable. We act out.

Have I ever been an insider? With my freedom I will never be "one of them"—a prisoner behind bars, but I am human, and so are they. We are all family. I, perhaps, can only help them realize it through my classes and by helping them write memories they have of the past. Who really is alien in our culture? Could the stranger be the prison staff? The prison professor? How can anyone stand in judgment? Petty or not, we are all guilty. We exist within physical and sociological entrapments—our concepts of freedom and staunch viewpoints—but these are all ideals we can *free* ourselves from if we are willing to *learn*.

I daydream that maybe I'll spot some of you, holding your children's hands, running your tattoo parlors, catfishing in your favorite holler holes, facing your demons the best you know how. I imagine a greeting from an aging mother who still relentlessly milks the Holsteins, imprisoned on her own farm, the smell of rotten silage and the overwhelming burden of not having enough time. She, though, will be waiting at her threshold, doors wide open for you. Imagine the toy brontosaurus on laminate flooring pointing its head to your childhood bedroom—you will be welcomed again. When you board that Greyhound bus to the halfway house, keep your head high. With smart time, you'll have only two months to go. Perhaps I played a part in some of this, here in this place any of us could have wound up in after a few misdirected decisions.

As kids, we were taught to never talk to a stranger. But who is he? The kid in junior high who helps you with your homework? The unfamiliar person who takes you safely to school? Who really knows?

I've been instructed never to get too close to any inmate. But I'm your teacher here, and I'm afraid that's just not possible. Tonight, like most nights, I carry you home.

Ooh Ra

IN REPLYING
REFER TO NO.

UNITED STATES MARINE CORPS

HEADQUARTERS
SIXTH MARINE DIVISION,
IN THE FIELD

In the name of the president of the United States, the Commanding General, Sixth Marine Division, takes pleasure in awarding the **BRONZE STAR MEDAL** to

CORPORAL CHARLES W. REESE
UNITED STATES MARINE CORPS RESERVE

for service as set forth in the following **CITATION**:

> "For the heroic achievement in connection with operations against the Japanese enemy on OKINAWA SHIMA, PYUKYU ISLANDS, on 8 June, 1945. While acting as a machine gun section leader of a Marine rifle company, Corporal REESE and one of his men were seriously wounded by enemy mortar fire…

The dimly lit hospice room has a long, narrow, fluorescent bulb on the wall above the headrest, a pull-chain for help, large buttons on the side of the bed for Emergency, a morphine drip, but no breathing machine—because Grampa Reese is still breathing on his own, even though his chest rises and falls at an ever slower rate. He hasn't spoken for the last day or two, but the nurses assure us he is still aware of everything and everyone around the room. Most of the time his eyes are closed. The heavy haze of impending death lingers. This is a man who helped raise you. You ask yourself as your mind races and flashes to the past, could you ever carry the weight he carried? This is blood, which by birth is your blood. Could you fight if your life depended on it? Could you ever be a hero?

> **...Fearing a likely enemy infiltration attempt, he did not want any of his men to leave the lines, so despite a severely lacerated foot, Corporal REESE crawled fifty yards on hands and knees to the platoon command post to seek aid for the other wounded man and to give valuable information as to the enemy situation at that time...**

The muted laminate flooring feels good under your feet. The faux-leather furniture is surprisingly roomy and comfortable—inviting you to sit down and try to rest for once in your life. There's contemporary art on the wall, a landscape from a generic location. It's someone's job to pick this artwork out—to make the final decision. No Edward Hopper's *Room in New York* or his *Excursion into Philosophy*, where an unhappy man dressed in business casual sits on the edge of a bed with a naked red-headed woman behind him and an open paperback next to him. If that painting were hanging in a hospice room a patient or visitor might start contemplating and asking—why the long face?

If you had your choice, you might pick Renoir's *Diana*—a naturalistic nude studio painting superimposed upon a contrived landscape. Renoir admitted the picture of his mistress was "considered pretty improper." He said he added the bow and the dead doe to transform his mistress into the ancient goddess of the hunt.

In the painting, the woman looks like she's got a little meat on her bones, which in the end would be comforting. You'd know you were in good hands. The woman can obviously kill with precision—in the nude, even. She likely knows how to butcher and dry some good venison. Probably has something buried deep in her dirt cellar, preserved for rainy days.

Diana the Huntress. How would she just appear here in flyover country? And really, what do you know about her or Renoir? Nothing except what you googled about the both of them. You laughed the first time you saw Diana the Huntress at the National Gallery of Art. That wasn't very chic of you. Later, after exhausting yourself moving room to room, you found yourself back in front of the painting. The whole family had long deserted you—they were tired of looking at art. You snapped a picture with your iPhone even though that's frowned upon. You knew you'd use it in something—isn't that what artists do? Steal from the best? Was this the best? It's what you remember most from that trip to the museums, trying to take it all in.

And Hopper. We have written so much about him, haven't we? He keeps pulling you back. You feel a little sophisticated because you know a bit of Hopper's history. In grad school you'd take your freshman composition classes to the Sheldon Memorial Art Gallery in Nebraska where you'd all stand in front of *Room in New York*—(29 inches x 36 inches). The curator told you how the gallery purchased the painting for $20,000 shortly after the artist completed it and that now it is worth enough to pay for you and all of your students' education. The painting is inexplicable. One of your friends wrote a song about Hopper painting sad and harsh colors. You both were in New York City for a bachelor party. You both snuck away from the bars to see Hopper's exhibit at the Guggenheim. All these men and their blank expressions: they can take it or leave it. That was a poisonous bachelor party. If you could go back in time, you might take it easy—ask yourself, *Why are we trying so hard to singe ourselves? Haven't we walked the thin line long enough? What are the givens?* It's too late. Or is it? You can't turn back the clocks. But *They is* time, just like Tobias Wolff mind chanted in "Bullet in the Brain," *they is, they is, they is.*

You're tired. Can't you stop thinking about yourself? How absurd is that thought at a time like this? Surely there's something you could be doing. The IV has run dry. Maybe the tubes have disconnected and need to be re-clamped—you sit alone waiting. For what? Answers, absolutes, a last-ditch effort. You start to recall textbook metaphors—*the whole world's a stage.* And similes—*time rushes by like a commuter late for work.*

...His courageous action undoubtedly saved the wounded man's life and materially aided his platoon in accomplishing its assigned task. His conduct was in keeping with the highest traditions of the United States Naval Service."

> LEMUEL C. SHEPHERD, JR.,
> Major General,
> U. S. Marine Corps

One time your neighbor stopped his lawnmower and said, "Today I was at work, then during lunch I found myself and a few dozen other people standing under one of those damn blue canopies in the cemetery. Then just like that, everyone had to head back to work. You know," he continued, "one thing you probably won't hear someone say when they're dying is, I wish I would have spent more time drinking, pissing the day away." Then your neighbor looked off into the bright sun and squinted and went back to mowing his yard.

Later that day, at home after leaving the hospice, you get word that Grampa passed. You ask yourself, are you always faithful? Are you always loyal? And although you know you will never have to go to war, you go searching in that shoebox for the bronze United States Marine Corps key-chain he gave you before you headed off into this world on your own. Your hands sweat as you cup the totem. You yearn Semper Fi. You shout, *Ooh Ra.*

My Life as Willy the Wildcat

I became Wayne State's mascot for all the wrong reasons. School spirit was not one of them. Teamwork; nope. I was silly. Willy the Wildcat. I was the guy behind the mask, inside an over-stuffed, thermal insulated sauna of a costume. I had pecs for the first time in my life. I was larger than life and people loved me. The seamstress who designed the costume went with a gender-neutral character—all smile and whiskers—for the kids. Underneath the straps, pads, and mask—inside the fur, it was me, all 120 pounds.

In their own serene way people always asked, "What does one have to do to become a mascot?" Or more bluntly they'd fire, "What?" "What were you thinking?" You know, I still don't mind the questions. Everyone, at some time, wouldn't mind jumping inside outside skin. And let's be honest, since I was a kid, I always wanted to have someone else's body. Not that mine was horrible, but I was weak and skinny. I never really had muscle. I daydreamed about other people's figures for about twenty years, until all of those people I secretly admired started to balloon in weight, lose their hair and become oddly disproportioned.

As the mascot, I was invited to the parties after the game. Every Saturday night was trick or treat for Willy—I was on the prowl. I always went, in costume of course. I was a riot. I was the life of the party. I could seriously dance my tail off. You know if you look up the word *mascot* in the dictionary, it says, "the one believed to bring good luck." I was determined to explore "luck's" facets to the extreme.

Picture a small northeast Nebraska town with a population of 8,000. Imagine Main Street running north and south from one end of town to the other—cobblestone and brick side streets still intact. This is Wayne, America, home of Chicken Days. This little island in northeast Nebraska would become another ghost town if it wasn't for the college and this yearly festival. Nevertheless, a lot of the locals spent the majority of their time complaining about the higher institution and the corruption it brought to the community. In essence, Wayne State was and still is a suitcase college—often students go back home to the family farm on the weekends to help out, or they make the two-hour trip south to Omaha, to "the big city." Thursday was and still is "party night." By the time Saturday's games roll around, students are gone.

When I was mascot, the football team didn't have a good year. The basketball team wasn't much better. I spent Saturdays in sparsely populated stadiums and gymnasiums, sometimes sleeping inside my costume. Full disclosure: the only highlight to these events was looking up through the air holes at the cheerleaders being held up in the air. I had a better view than anyone else. No one could tell where I was looking—it was straight up and always with a big smile. Don't let any male cheerleader tell you they never looked. We were young men who learned about sex by watching movies like *16 Candles, Weird Science* and *Risky Business*. We were a group of eighteen, nineteen and twenty-year-olds whose emotional intelligence wasn't fully developed. We were high-strung on hormones. Women looked at other women, too. On more than one occasion I overheard, "Did you see Veronica's thong? What a ho." Half the guys on the squad were there specifically to get to know the cheerleaders better. And some of them did. We were a tight-knit and eclectic group of characters with an odd sense of school spirit.

The mascot job was serious business. I was to represent my college on and off campus. More than once, I jogged the length of Wayne, America and back. Up and down Main Street from the campus to the outer city limits for parades and festivities. My motto should have been, "Have costume, will run." The town itself had lost its school spirit. As much as the locals complained about the college they still rallied around Wayne State when they were winning. "Who else do I have to root for around here?" was something I heard with a sad kind of chuckle on a few occasions. They were fair-weather fans, which was quite evident. And because of the town's size and the narrow-minded mentality of some, being the town pick-me-up could be difficult. I didn't quite understand the dynamics of small town America, but I was learning quickly. The scratch-my-back mentality worked well, until there was a problem or something failed to matriculate, and then people's attitudes quickly turned to brighter and shinier pastures on a dime.

How did I get the gig? The school was hard up, really. And by word of mouth I heard from another male cheerleader in my dorm that the position was open. And for some reason, this new proposition intrigued me. I saw myself as a star on and off the field—wherever I went, people would be talking about me. It was an early disillusionment and eagerness that seemed to come so naturally for me.

I never got too involved in high school like so many other people I knew. High school was such a large part of their identity, then and now. High school for me was a non-monumental wash. All I cared about at that time was Kate Johnson, what was under her plaid Catholic skirt, and my guitar. I sure as hell didn't give a hoot about playing sports and didn't have much school spirit. Picking a college wasn't hard. My father came downstairs one night where I was fiddling with some new chord-progression on my acoustic Alvarez and asked if I had thought about college. The band in which I played rhythm guitar and sang a few songs incredibly out of key had performed at Wayne State that year for their first Earth Day celebration. So I told him yeah, I thought Wayne State looked good. And that was that.

Upon arriving at the college, I remember my father saying, "I'll guarantee you'll find something to get involved with here. Sky's the limit, kid." Deep down inside, I did want to please my parents. I wanted to be more than just a mediocre kid who could kind of play the guitar. I wasn't a prodigy. I wasn't that athletic. I could ollie pretty high on a skateboard, but couldn't ride a half-pipe. I was writing these incredibly bad poems that I thought would stand the test of time. I wasn't quite pushing myself to my full potential. I had an excessive knowledge of music. Had long, wavy, pretty hair. I was good at posing, but I really wanted and needed to do something with some conviction. I wanted to stand out. Besides trying to please my parents, I actually thought the costume might benefit me in more than one way. I actually thought it might help me find a date—or, perhaps, even, a girlfriend with whom I could share my poetry.

I met the seven member cheer-squad in a fluorescent-lit practice area inside the field house. All the cheerleaders seemed alert and giddy. I felt like I was in a room full of people high-strung on Mountain Dew and white crosses. I was nervous. I figured if I blew mascot tryouts that would be the end of amounting to anything. In my mind, I had pictured a long line of us ready to try out. At least ten people, right? I was unaware of the school's athletic record, though. It was only me and a guy from Wyoming, who already had previous experience. We both listened and waited to try out while Kari, the cheer squad captain, laid out the ground rules. Kari was a fifth-year-senior squad leader. I'd seen her parading around campus in her cheerleading outfit before. It was something I had grown accustomed to in high school, but here it seemed a bit odd. She always wore the college's home colors—a black skirt pulled up a little too high. Her black and gold spandex top was fitting and snug.

"Being Willy is a privileged position here at Wayne State. Go Wildcats! Not only are you representing all of us as a team, you are representing Wayne State. Woo!" It was virtually impossible for Kari to say Wayne State without a weeping cheer.

"There will be times when you are expected to go above and beyond your call of duty. Every parade in town, the school's alumni picnics, the town hall Halloween trick for tots—you are expected to be present at all of these special events. It's tradition. And this year, if we play our cards right, Wayne State has promised to reimburse us. They have promised to pay for all of our textbooks for the fall and spring semesters. Woo!"

I heard Wyoming mumble, "Screw this. Picnics. Trick for tots."

"Yeah," I tissed under my breath.

"Willy the frigging Wildcat," Wyoming said. "Shit, I'm a Newcastle Dogie. I don't need this."

To be honest, I was relieved. I didn't want to face the fact that I might be a failure at mascot tryouts. Athletically, this was my last straw. When I found out he had been a mascot before, I was truly intimidated. But now, I knew I had him beat. I knew that Wyoming didn't have the attitude and spunk necessary to carry out such expectations. I made eye contact with Kari, smiled and nodded every time she barked out orders.

"Go Cats!" I hollered.

"Oh, I'm sorry," Kari said sadly. "Willy can't talk."

We took turns trying out. I had to stand out in the hallway while Mr. Dogie, the motherless calf that he was, strutted his stuff. When it was my turn, I was instructed to put Willy's mask on and excite the audience for three minutes. The mask was large in circumference and size, barely resting on my puny shoulders. It smelled awfully foul. My eyes watered the first time I put it on.

"The key," Kari said, "is to keep Willy's head from falling off during stunts and routines. Now let's see you shake that thang!" Kari hollered as the music pumped through a large boom box. *You all ready for this…*

I peered through the enormous grin that was Willy's mouth. Through the dark mesh I could barely make out figures and shapes. The bass of the stereo was kicking, and I began to pop a few locks—my arms and body took on a life of their own; I was gyrating to the music and clawing at the air. I began to juke and jive and a slow, predatory, animalistic stutter-step followed. What would Willy do? I thought. I compensated for my lack of a tail and mimed imaginary actions, got on all fours, arched my back and frolicked with positions that were downright dirty. Every once in a while, as I tried to catch my breath in this new mask (and body of mine) I peered over my shoulder at the crowd of cheerleaders—egging them on for something more than just a tailspin. If I could have, I would have licked my whiskers and lips—would have roared—but that was against the rules. I'm not sure why simulating an animal brings out sexualized behaviors in others, in me, and I didn't care. I mean, really, aren't we all animals with a few quirks and characteristics that tell us apart from the herd?

After the first minute, I knew I had them. I might as well have been calling up the spirits, I was *back in the animal kingdom*. When the music finished, I was already soaking inside the mask. I had managed to work up an incredible sweat and thirst for more. I knew appetite was the road to life and culture. A few of the male cheerleaders came over and sized me up. Kari instructed Guss, one of the male co-leaders, to toss me in the air. I put my right foot in his hands, grabbed hold of my wildcat ears, and was airborne. He and another cheerleader caught me, and for a second, cradled me like a new-born child.

"Hell, he can't weigh more than a buck-fifteen, sopping wet," Guss said.

"Good. Good!" Kari squealed. "Bring the other guy in. Before we make our final decision, we have a few questions for you. For the next few minutes we will be referring to you both as Willy—okay?"

"Okay!"

"Let's say a young child is lost and is looking for mommy or daddy. Nine times out of ten the child will come to you, Willy—you are a familiar face. What will you say to this little boy or girl?"

"I thought we couldn't talk," Wyoming said.

I gave Kari a look of alarm and knew this was my chance to seal the deal. "I would calm the little fella," I said. "And reassure her or him that they are safe with me. Immediately, I would take the child to the proper authorities."

"Great answer, Willy! On occasions like this it is okay to talk—safety is the number one concern for our little wildcats."

I gave Wyoming a look of triumph.

"Prick," he mumbled.

"Okay, we'll need a few minutes to make our final decision," Kari said.

"You're a little pecker, you know that?" Wyoming said. I didn't say a word. I knew I had this cat in the bag.

I was skinny. I thought I was funny. I was easy to toss into the air and catch. I wasn't afraid to get dropped on the ground, and I was wiry and high-strung, and that's what got me the job.

For a while, I took the job seriously. I was incognito. The cheerleaders called me Willy in and out of costume. My biggest fans were kids who asked a million questions and followed me around like I was Mother Goose, yanking on my tail and kicking and hitting me in the privates. That was the hardest part of the job. Dealing with little snot-nosed peckers whose moms had dumped them off at the stadium for the day. "Go play with Willy" were words I learned to despise. When I wasn't being thrown in the air or rattled by these little pipsqueaks, I was busy trying to hit on women.

I was a big cuddly cat and I took full advantage of every situation I could. We all are animalistic—it's human nature. Was exterior-Willy really what women wanted? I was destined to find out. Deep down inside, did they want me to leave the costume on, keep hold of my head and at the very last moment rip my head off and…?

"Come sit on my lap, Willy," one woman propositioned. "Who's under that big furry mask?" another purred. Game nights required nothing more than simulating an animal—paw petting and hip thrusts. I could feign a cat-crawl on all fours—my back in perfect alignment with the horizon and sunset I was hell-bent for. I believed I really knew how to take my time. I was instructed not to talk and that seemed to suit women just fine. On one occasion, a frisky lady friend asked me back into a dorm room—costume and all. The problem with that, once the enormous head was removed, was that she discovered I was nothing more than a sweaty little man. My head barely protruded from my enormous shoulder pads. It was dark in her room, aside from a small reading lamp by her bed. As I looked over my breast-pads I could see her on her tip toes looking in.

"Oh Willy, it's okay," she said.

"I think I had too much to drink."

The "lady friend" somehow managed to look past the fact that she wanted to screw around with a stuffed cat. Oh, the dreams, disguises and fantasies we impose on other people will continue to baffle me. Immediately after my papier-mâché head came off, her hysterical laughter and sighs ensued. I felt used and embarrassed, and I hadn't even taken my *real* clothes off.

CatMan was my self-proclaimed sidekick. He was a junior undeclared-major who dressed in shiny black tights and wore a cape with a dysfunctional capital C stitched on the back. The whole costume looked like something he'd thrown together when he was in grade school. CatMan stood tall and proud at six feet, three inches. His cape barely touched his rump. The eyeholes in his homemade mask were cut out and crooked. His mustache protruded from the hole he hollered out of. He talked—yelled on many occasions, leaving fans a bit uncomfortable at times. It was makeshift at best, but as far as I was concerned, it was brilliant. No other mascot had a partner in crime, at least none I'd seen. He strapped his own pair of shiny black tights on, and he wasn't afraid to let it all hang out.

He took the liberty of talking for the both of us. He'd been at this charade for three years and was determined to see the football team to a winning season before he graduated—that was his goal. The first half of the game, he was always high on school spirit and hope. The second half, imagine a cokehead out of town without dope. He would work himself into a frenzy. He took the game more seriously than any fan. We'd both take a smoke break at the beginning of the fourth quarter in the greens-keeper's shed. In between our drags, we'd try to contemplate plans—something to rile and stimulate the crowd.

"I don't know why we do it, Willy. Parading around here like some lunatics, and where's the love, tell me, where's the love? Everyone here, a bunch of spoil sports. What this team needs is a goddamn pick-me-up!"

I'd shrug my shoulders, but I'm not sure he could ever tell. And it went on like this for about ten minutes while we hot-boxed Marlboros and chugged Gatorade, or until some little dipstick popped his head inside the greens-keeper's shed and went off running and screaming, "Willy and CatMan are smoking! Willy is smoking!" Our intentions, for the most part, were honorable. I liked to believe the teams were, too.

I remember phoning my dad after I had participated in a few games, to tell him the good news. To tell him his son had finally gotten involved in sports. After I relayed the information—a long pause ensued and I heard my father choke on something. I probably couldn't tell then if he was laughing or choking.

"Here, why don't you talk to your mother," is all he said.

I told my mother the good news, too, and she said nothing.

"Mom," I asked, "Are you there?"

"Yes, Dear, I was just finishing off a glass of wine." She questioned everything I had just told her, pretending, like usual, that I had made the story up.

"So what is all this mascot business you're talking about? Jumping and parading around like some kind of animal. Is it part of the theatre program or something?" I heard my father burst out laughing; this time it was clearly evident that he wasn't choking. I could hear my mother cover the receiver with her hand.

"Stop it, Mike, he's our son." She had muffled the phone, but she and my father's conversation had come through clear enough.

"That's great, honey. We'll be up soon to see you on Parent's Day. Go Wildcats!" I heard the two of them laugh together as she hung up the phone.

A couple of weeks later, my parents made the two-hour trip north with a group of their friends to see the Wayne State Wildcats play. It was a picture-perfect day and, during the first half, the Cats weren't doing too badly, either. CatMan and I juiced up our routine, and I had the guys throw me around a few extra times so that my parents could see that this mascot business was more than just fun and games. It took precision and skill. Landings could be treacherous, but not this day. They might see exterior-Willy—this big, dumb, stuffed costume, doing stupid stuff—but inside I was more than their socially inept son, I was Willy the friggin' Wildcat, baby, and I truly believed I had found my calling. At least for the time being. This was something worthwhile. I was sophisticated and suave. I was learning to use my body without using my big mouth, which was odd and gratifying for once in my life. I could enjoy this freedom for a long afternoon once a week.

During halftime, there was a lot to do and see. The local FFA chapter even auctioned off some pigs during the halftime extravaganza. CatMan and I had a front row seat next to the chute where they loaded and unloaded the boars. As the auction proceeded, so did my confusion about the whole process—I didn't know if the pigs were coming or going. Somewhere along the line I had slipped and fallen into some pig excrement. I hoped my parents didn't see this. I hoped no one would see this. People do pay more attention to you when you are a large stuffed animal, but it's not like all eyes are on you. My ensuing panic may have been uncalled for. I spent the rest of the game trying to get the crap off my fur—trying to play it cool.

I met my folks in the parking lot after the game. They had managed to concoct an elaborate tailgating party for themselves, their friends, and a group of other festive parents. They had done a fine job polishing off a Coors party ball. I'm not sure how much of the game they'd seen. During halftime, I saw my mother wave to me and snap a few pictures with a disposable camera. But, come to think of it, I never did see my father or his friends after the first quarter.

"So, what did you think?" I asked. "I mean, it wasn't my best performance, but all in all, I gave it a good run today. My landing during the third quarter was a little off, but I'm still trying to compensate for this enormous head."

"What did you say the record was for these guys?" asked one of my father's canoe buddies as he took a pull of whiskey from a pocket-pint. "They sure blow."

"Something smells like crap. Can anyone smell that?" another parent said.

"Hey, good work today, kid. You got a lot of spirit." My father had his arm around me and was kind of slurring his words. Or maybe I was hyper-analyzing the situation. Had I become worthwhile enough for my parents? I wasn't sure how much more involved in college I could get. I was never going to be a good athlete. Maybe I could try a club sport, but this was as far as I'd get to suiting up and taking the field in any NCAA Division II sport. I was morphing inside my costume—the parents suave with alcohol, their own temporary disguise—the lens zooming in, looking pretty sharp for the moment.

"Hey, let's get a picture. Hey, you guys, get over here, let's take a picture with my son, Willy." Me, CatMan, and a group of parents posed for pictures as the remainder of the crowd moseyed into the stadium parking lot.

Rivals of Wayne State College are the University of Nebraska-Kearney Lopers. According to Kari, it was tradition that we make the trip southwest for their homecoming. Willy on a road trip? Hell, yes! I'd never been to Kearney, and the thought of getting out of "Wayne, America" for the weekend pleased me. By the time we arrived on Friday night, the party was well underway.

So, it went. The frat boys with their blue school colors and khaki pants kept mixing and pouring a concoction they called "Loper Piss." It was a blue-green Kool-Aid mix they served out of a blue Coleman cooler with wheels. The partygoers would add ice from time to time, and whatever Everclear, vodka, gin or white liquor people brought with them. Someone would add sugar and blue Kool-Aid from time to time. As the night progressed, rumor spread that I was the team mascot. And, to my surprise, I was welcomed with open arms. At one point, I remember hugging and dancing with Kari. By ten o-clock—*Happy Hour*, everyone had mustaches and purple tongues. It was liquid candy, and most of us over-indulged.

"Fuel Man! Fuel Man! Willy needs more Loper Piss!" I roared.

"More Loper Piss for Willy!"

"Don't mind if I do."

We were staying at a friend's house who was on the UNK wrestling team; a "good guy" who wouldn't let anything happen to his friends from WSC. Around midnight, I was coerced into taking Willy's head out of its protective traveling case—a black heavy-duty 33-gallon Glad trash bag. Our friend paraded around his house with the mask on. It was odd to watch someone else crawl inside my costume. Willy was acting on his own behalf without consulting with me. He was being unfaithful. I was in no shape to entertain the masses at this point but I was beginning to feel a bit betrayed the more I watched. He took to the front porch, then the street screaming profanities to our opponents. "You're the only one that understands me," he said, holding a can of Budweiser in front of Willy's face, talking to the can. Didn't he know Willy wasn't supposed to say anything?

The head fit him well. At 6' 3" he was a natural. No one talked back to him. But even in my drunken haze, I knew this wasn't a good idea. My disguise had divorced me and I could see repercussions coming.

Kari insisted throughout the night that we arrive at the field an hour early to practice routines and get what few WSC fans who were there "pumped up!" Her dedication and enthusiasm for the squad was never dulled—not even after rounds of Loper Piss. And we had all put down our guards. I was starting to fall for her and the booze helped me realize how important our jobs were. "Hell, yes!" I slur-roared again. "Take it to the field."

Come morning, the cheer squad left were hurting units. I wanted to stay in the corner I'd curled up in and lick my wounds. Besides, I wasn't getting paid for this. My textbooks the college promised to pay for hadn't come through, either. All of this became much clearer to me as I cracked open the nearest warm beer. My inner voice kept telling me to stand up for myself. And to boot, CatMan wasn't along to pick me up. I had to go at this game alone. I was struggling to remember how the night ended. As I went into the john, I saw Willy's head propped on top of the toilet. The rest of the costume was still in the trash bag. I finished the warm beer and found another—hair of the cat.

I was late. I could hear the drum corps from the front porch and knew the stadium couldn't be that far away. The rest of the place was empty except for a few stragglers and Guss, who had been hugging a corner of the living room, too. There was a guy smoking next to what was left of the Loper Piss.

I finished the beer, found some aspirin and my toothbrush.

What I wore under the costume was shorts and a t-shirt. I strapped my breasts and shoulder pads on—which took some time since CatMan wasn't around to help me, and the only cheerleader left was passed out. I crawled inside the long-sleeved fur coveralls—found my gloves and fur booties. I pulled the long-sleeved black and gold jersey over the coveralls. I felt light-headed, but knew I had to go if I was to get a ride back to Wayne, America. I kicked Guss on the way out.

"She said put that furry thing away," he said strangely and happily.

By the time I made it to the stadium, I was drenched. The head smelled like a locker room. And the Loper Piss was seeping out of me. Every once in a while, someone would holler, "WSC sucks!" Like I'd never heard that before. Through Willy's mouth I could make out the parking lot, and I managed to spot the wrestler and some images I remembered from the night before. There was a continuous thumping coming from the lower back of my real head. They immediately waved me over. Pre-game, as I was about to find out, consisted of red beers and Bloody Marys. Before long, my head was off and the drinking ensued.

"Hot damn, Willy. Top of the morning to you!" the wrestler said.

After two Bloody Marys and one tomato beer, I regained my muscles. I was getting looks from some of the WSC fans who had made the trip and happened to pass me, headless, with my tail hanging out. The first quarter was well underway, and I had decided I ought to go down to the game. I wandered down to the track that surrounded the football field. The true beauty of that costume were days like this. Doors and gates magically opened for me. Through Willy's mouth, I could make out the homecoming crowd, which was much larger than I had anticipated. People actually showed up for football games in Kearney. I spotted Kari and the rest of the crew.

"Willy's here!" Kari exclaimed. She gave me a big bear hug and grabbed my ass. I was confused—why was she being so nice to me? She came in close and purred in my ear. What couldn't I remember from the night before? I gave the squad a wave and turned to the dance floor. We were down by fourteen points already, and it wasn't even halftime. The next play, WSC intercepted a pass and took the ball downfield for a touchdown.

"Ready!"

Boom Chucka Boom Chucka Boom Boom Boom!

"Here we go Wildcats!" *Boom Chucka* "Here we go!"

We made the extra point, and some people in the crowd actually cheered. Our drummers continued to rattle and boom as I did my best to jive and shake. Tyrone and Billy grabbed and hoisted me above their heads. They gave me a jolt, and I was airborne. I could feel my gut rise—that same feeling you have at the crest of a large hill, while road-tripping in a car on hilly terrain. Some of the red beer came out my nose. My balance and equilibrium were shot—the landing was ugly. Tyrone laughed and picked me up off the ground.

"Shake it off, Willy," he said. If he only knew.

I realized I had to lose it but I hadn't puked since I was a freshman in high school, when my father forced me to drink four Big Gulps of water until the booze came out—I swore then, I'd never over-indulge again. I ran to the side of the grandstands to get some air. I threw the mask off and started dry-heaving. The ground was spinning. I wanted out—everything—the booze, this lousy costume, Kari's hands on my ass—maybe college. Nothing was what it seemed.

"Honey, I think that mascot is drunk," I heard some Loper fan say. "Maybe we should report him."

I had to regain my composure. I took some deep breaths and slowly danced my way back to the cheerleaders. I patted a few kids on the head for good measure. When I got back to the cheer squad, things had quieted down a bit. Everyone sat crossed-legged on the ground. I joined them. The ground was spinning. It was hard to stay focused on anything. I closed my eyes and prayed that the game would end soon.

One of the cheerleaders hollered, "Hey, Willy, look at that mascot over there. Go make a friend."

"Why don't you go make a friend?" I piped back.

Off in the distance, I spotted the seven-foot antelope. Our costumes were similar, but from here I could already see he was going to tower over me. Beside him were four shirtless guys in football helmets with horns and shorts. And, all at once, they started sprinting in my direction. The Loper's head bouncing up and down and the shirtless guys with fists waving in the air—it didn't look good. But this was a family affair after all. What could really go wrong?

I got up. Whatever they had planned, I wasn't going to sit down. I hollered at Tyrone, but he pretended not to hear me. I remember thinking, what are they really going to do?—we are school mascots, after all. A whistle blew, and I ran onto the field towards them—trying to play good sport. I was right—as the

Loper approached—he towered over me. The four guys grew louder and I made out a few of their words.

"Hey, bitch. You're not so funny now!" the Loper said. "Now's when we start kicking your ass!" One of the shirtless football players added. I turned and tried to run. There was an obvious mistake in identity.

And, so it went. The Loper tackled me at a running sprint. My breast pads protected the fall, for the most part. I had the papier-mâché mask on to protect my head, but it was loose and the kicks to it dug into my neck and shoulder blades. What I remember being worried about the most was what every guy fears in this situation. I curled up into a fetal position as soon as I could manage and cupped my nuts while the rest of the guys took pop-shots at my ribs and tailbone, pummeling my ass. As big as they were, it still didn't hurt like you'd imagine it would, like in the movies. I lay there for what seemed like a long time—my whole body thumping and being thumped. But it went faster than you'd expect—the Loper looking on—hands raised.

"Eat that, Willy!" he shouted down to me before they all ran off. "You aren't as tough as your were last night—huh!"

I suppose looking back on it all now, it's a bit comical. All along I wanted people to see Willy and I as the same—to feel welcomed and accepted. By putting on my mask, I truly believed I was transforming into the character I always believed I should be.

For instance, I remember vividly standing outside of the "Party House" on 5th and Pearl in Wayne, America for our homecoming festivities. I was outside, likely trying to bum a free beer or was thinking of running from the cops who always busted the parties. Either way, I'm positive I was trying to act cool. What I remember so clearly, probably because it shattered the ego I was working so hard on, was walking up to people and introducing myself as Willy the Wildcat. There was one girl I was sweet on—everyone was sweet on. One of the football players kept egging me on to ask her out—so I tried. After I energetically introduced myself, "Hey, I'm Willy the Wildcat, your school mascot!" She looked me up and down and said, "You're something, all right." It was a major blow to my self-esteem. The ego I was growing accustomed to. The Wildcats were on a losing streak, and I was stuck as the pipsqueak school mascot for an entire year. "Come on, Willy," I remember the football player saying, "Let's go find you a big, big beer."

I can only imagine one of our daughters calling home her first year of college—telling us she is the new school mascot—the town clown. But I'll be cool about it. I mean, after all, I was Willy the frigging Wildcat '91-'92. I mean, no one else can say that. If you think I wouldn't support my girls, you're crazy. After watching my oldest daughter jump and tumble and attempt a handstand while kicking a leg out to her side like a helpless dog, I bought her professional pom-poms for her 3rd birthday. She might not be San Diego Chicken material yet, but I have my hopes.

Ready—Action!

I'm standing in line at the mega-pharmacy, waiting to buy drugs. I know, I don't like this place either, but it's handy and cheap. Standing in this slow line, I can't keep my eyes off the prophylactic section. Two young guys with bottles of 5-Hour Energy shrug shoulders, laugh, turn to look at who might be staring at them, joke louder, turn back to the KY and rows of Trojans and Lifestyles while they fondle the Astroglide. This is where they come for all their necessities—frozen pizza, toilet paper, ammunition.

"Don't be such a numb-nut," one says to the other as they snicker and turn their cart down the aisle. Soon enough they're back, intent this time on grabbing the right product. I want to tell them about my very own raging young libido—a firecracker with a short fuse ready to pop. I had a years-old condom back then that I never had the nerve to use when the occasion presented itself, and the only result was a permanent round shadow on my wallet. So good for you guys. Way to be proactive—or active. You will never be more ready and randy than you are right now—so profit from it. But, of course, I don't say anything. I don't want to be that creepy guy.

Then off they go, burying their goods in a large half-empty cart that in a couple of years they will fill with formula, baby wipes, diapers, Aquaphor Healing Ointment, Clorox disinfectant wipes, lead paint test kits (because their wives will read too many *Parenting* magazines and begin freaking out about lead lurking in everything). Soon, they will fill the cart with various hand sanitizers for every room in the house and the new fanny pack they carry with them but refuse to wear. They will add lots of sugar-free juice, binkies, tearless shampoo, a Pack and Play, a plastic tote (for hoarding their concert lighters, favorite sneakers and t-shirts)—a bouncy seat, pregnancy tests, a bottle warmer, colored condoms, acid reducers, Band-Aids, Ativan, peroxide, and tonic.

The cart will overflow. That will only be the beginning.

Today, though, none of that stuff matters. They race for the only male check-out clerk who, God willing, will let them pass through, accepting their hard-earned cash without asking for their IDs or whether they need to speak with the pharmacist about practical application, correct procedures, or any other instruction they've never wanted or been given.

All I Need is a Remedy to Cool

Kelly used to lean against the brick pillar in the commons area. Kelly with a "Y" not an "I." No one made fun of him because he was named after a girl. He was bald except for his brown, sixteen-inch Mohawk, perfectly sprayed with some kind of industrial Aqua Net. This was circa 1989, 1990. He was the living myth—the embodiment of cool. He was two years older than I was, kept to himself and his *bitchin'* girlfriend who we didn't dare stare at. She was exotic, and we yearned for her as much as we ached to be Kelly.

He had his swagger and bounce. Black leather jacket, jeans tucked into black combat-boots. Every once in a while, he had a spiral notebook or a novel in his hand. None of us read for fun until we saw him do it, then we did. What was he reading? How'd he get his biceps to pop like they did? Were those song lyrics in his notebook? No one saw him at the gym. No one saw him on any open-mike stage. No one saw him anywhere outside of school, because he was Kelly and he was *Motherfucking Cool*.

After the school bell rang, he went to some superior place we didn't have directions to or could have found if we'd wanted. I tried reaching with my pre-grunge, punk rock, metal collective. I had Z. Cavarrici pants, a Misfits t-shirt, checkered Vans, and long, wavy hair my mom had permed for me and which I bleached with peroxide. Six months after idolizing him, I bought a black leather biker-jacket and had all the faces of Metallica painted on the back. A year after that, I stripped them off and had my friend paint an enormous picture of Marilyn Monroe in their place. If her nostalgic paraphernalia sales were doing so well, surely the royalties had to rub off on me. Once I was a junior, Kelly was gone. He graduated. Someone said he was too cool to walk during the ceremony, but we didn't attend and never knew for sure.

Twenty-nine years later, I'm thinking about you, Kelly. How I imagine some inimitable people flash back to us. How I am trying to tell my daughter, who has car keys now, how important it is to find her own voice. But how do we know who to model or avoid? I never truly knew you, Kelly. You were distant, and I was naïve and ill-informed. Maybe you could see this. Maybe I only imagined the raddest song lyrics in your notebook. Maybe I only imagined your confidence. You walked through doors with your head up, your shoulders never slouched. That's what I saw. But what did I know?

I slouched through doors. I made jokes, and people laughed, but they didn't know me either. I ran my hand through my hair and laughed, too. But my daughter could use your myth, and I still, even now, want to believe it myself. So, when I see my daughter again in the kitchen I begin to tell her the story of you. "Back in high school there was this guy, Kelly. Man he was cool."

I start my third sentence when she interrupts and says, "Whatever."

Sasquawk and Copenhagen

I spent five years in college in Wayne, a small northeast
Nebraska town. "Wayne America" still adorns the area water tower.
I was twenty-one and had just been fired from the local watering
hole. I had only bartended a few nights before the locals petitioned
to ban me permanently from behind the bar. It was the mid-nineties
and, like a few of my friends, I grew my hair long and tied flannel
shirts around my waist. Some of the patrons called me "stoner."

One night, after too many whiskey presses, Harry Ferguson, a
Spanked Dog Pub regular, whose motor skills and vision had been
altered, confused me for a woman. "She's a looker, alright," he said,
loud enough for his drinking buddies to hear. "Harry. She's a guy!"
After the commotion simmered down and he regained his footing
at the bar, Harry spent the rest of the night throwing insults at me.
"We got ourselves a live one here. I bet he rows from both sides of
his canoe." The next day, I got my walking papers.

"Besides," the owner of the Spanked Dog said, "You wanna be
a writer. I hear the *Herald* is looking for a good writer. I can't have
Harry confusing you for a woman, falling off his stool. Without
these guys I'd go broke. You understand?"

He handed me fifty bucks, and I walked, literally across the alley,
to the weekly paper. What the hell, I thought. I'll be broke soon
enough, and yes, I wanted to become a writer.

I sat across from the editor-in-chief. He wore a bow tie. It went
well with his Burt Reynold's mustache. His name was Dwayne.
The plaques, press awards, and diplomas on the wall behind him
immediately grabbed my attention. He was generous with my first
assignment and gave me rein to buck it out. He handed me an
address, no phone number, and scribbled a name down on a piece
of paper—Edgar. I didn't know what to expect. I didn't have any

questions prepared since I didn't know what the assignment was. I didn't think to ask, either. I went home and grabbed a pen and pad of paper. My father had given me a leather high-dollar folder with a lock that he received free from some actuarial firm that was trying to court him. I grabbed that—seemed appropriate. There was nothing to it, really.

I rang the doorbell and, when a guy answered, I told him I was there to do the story. He sat me down and started talking. I would write my first article about Edgar Smith, a 72-year-old cyclist who had biked across the United States in one summer—for the third time in his life. I jotted down important days the guy remembered— windy terrain through the Rocky Mountains; home cooking at area hostels; a flat tire in Indiana, and so forth. I looked at maps and photos for a couple of hours until his wife made me stay for dinner. We had goulash, green beans, homemade bread and rhubarb pie for dessert. I hadn't eaten that well in months.

I chose some Creedence Clearwater Revival lyrics in honor of the man's accomplishments as the headline: *Big Wheel Keep on Turnin.'*

I felt good about the article and had a Ziploc bag of photos the guy had given me to show to my boss. I had to return them immediately, unharmed after the article was finished.

Dwayne read the article I had worked up, shook his head, and kept looking over the top of his glasses in my direction. Then he said, "You know you wrote this entire piece of crap in first person?"

"Oh," I said. "You mean you want me to take out the part about us eating goulash."

"Yes, I want you to take it out. No one cares that you ate goulash with the guy!" Dwayne hollered.

Like every good editor, he handed me the piece and told me to do it over. The next day, after he'd approved my revision, he was eager to dole out more assignments. I quickly learned whose voice to capture in the stories—nobody's. From Izaak Walton fish fries to the Annual Chicken Show's egg drop, I covered the weekly realm of current events in Wayne, America.

The city chamber started the Wayne Chicken Show in the early eighties, and according to the brochures scattered around town, chose the theme of "chickens" because *1) chickens are artful; 2) most people have knowledge and familiarity with chickens; and, 3) chickens can be considered with humor.* I knew nothing about chickens, except that my father always overcooked them, and they were usually dry and served smothered with gravy. When Crazy Craig attached a 12- foot fiberglass rooster to the top of his '67 Cadillac Coupe DeVille for the town's yearly parade, I was there to break the story. In a few simple steps, I can tell you how to hypnotize a chicken. Ira

Bloomburg draws three lines in the dirt—two to hold the chicken steady and one to hypnotize it. You keep that bird's eyes fixated on all three of those lines; after about a minute it won't move.

I can tell you how the town gobbles up mass quantities of the bird in its many varieties—there's fried chicken, chicken fried chicken, chicken on a stick, barbequed chicken, chicken nuggets, and the fallback: Martha Goodbar's half a roasted chicken and some fixin's. Wayne, America would double and sometimes triple in size, people coming from around the Plains and from some big cities to pay homage to Sasquawk, the Chicken Coupe, and to the Chickendale dancers—a group of overweight male Caucasians with decorative brown bags covering their heads and dancing atop a flatbed trailer wearing nothing more than boxer shorts or spandex.

Aside from the annual chicken show, I occasionally ventured outside of the town limits to meet farmers and ranchers who really made up the county. In doing so, I had a better understanding of where I had landed. Although I wouldn't know what a JD 3020 was, I decided that when I got back to the office, I'd look it up or corral someone into a confession. A tractor—why didn't the guy just say so, I thought. I was the paper's greenhorn. They all got a lot of laughs on my behalf. Whatever needed to be done, I did. I worked on stories and interviews while the pipsqueak sports editor and Dwayne played golf. I didn't care. I was trying to indulge in as much writing as I could.

Then one day Dwayne came to me and said he had a special assignment. He told me that the most important thing about journalism was delivering the paper to the people. And he was short on drivers and needed me to fill in. I obliged, of course, and got stuck in the back of the print shop stacking papers as they came off the printer. After that, I'd have to bundle the things and learn how to label them. Lastly, I would drive bags of breaking news to Pilger, Hoskins, Stanton, and Norfolk, Nebraska.

Randy, a toothless and haggard looking grunt in his fifties, was my supervisor once a week as I wrapped and bundled and labeled and brought the news to the people.

"Now, over here," Randy hollered, "the first thing you've got to do is tie these here like this—on both sides. Otherwise, the papers will come loose, and you'll lose them, and they won't stand for that at the Post. This tie-er is tricky. You've gotta play with her. Hell, give her a name if you want. Last fella called her Betty. Said it worked better for him that way. Anyhow, if it gets tangled, you gotta go in with your hands and pull it out. And if that don't work, then you're gonna have to get some pliers. And trust me, you'll need some. I got a pair you can use for today, but come next week, you better have your own. See. Rips right out like this. She's just a bitch to re-string is all, and there is no time to reload her when the papers come pouring in."

Randy had bent over to show me the whole operation, and the crack of his ass was exposed. I tried to stay focused. The machine. What would I call her?

"Now over here you got your bags. Hook 'em here. It makes it easier so you don't have to mess with throwing 'em in by hand. Each bag's got a label, too. You got your Pilger Route, Pilger City, here. You got your Hoskins, Randolph, Crofton, and Wynot over here. And you have to circle Wynot's. Don't ask why—all's I know is they'll send them back, and then you'll have to drive them out there in the morning, and they'll already be late. LaVerta Hughes—she'll bitch because she didn't read it first-hand. And all it really is is a circle. So don't forget!"

Who the hell was LaVerta Hughes, and who gives a rip? I thought. Nothing in those newspapers was earth-shattering. I knew. I was writing the articles. National news came days late, if at all.

"Yer Hartington and Laurel go over here. Same with Ponca! Don't forget to circle them, too. If you think it needs a circle, circle it—hell, circle them all, for all I care. Otherwise, they'll send them back like the baglickers in Wynot. Bastards can't figure out to just look if it ain't labeled right. All the ones from Wayne go on this cart. And listen—they're priority number UNO. They have to be at the post office by 6:00. They like them earlier, but 6:00 is the latest. Any later and they'll leave without 'em, and then you're screwed. I wouldn't even come back to work if that happens."

Randy stopped. Looked at me and dug his left hand in his back pocket and pulled out a can of Copenhagen. In one scoop he had his dip. He tapped it on the can—careful not to lose much grain. He slopped it in his bottom lip. All the while, he didn't take his eyes off me, nor did I take my eyes off him—my new cancer-mouthed boss. He sucked in and swallowed.

"When you drop off the papers, you have to give them this envelope, otherwise it's not authorized. They want their money first— of course. Close them all up tight. Load 'em—Wayne on this side and the others on the other side. That way, you can differentiate. And no smoking in the truck. In case of some accident we only got liability, so be careful."

Randy spit, made me give him his pliers back, and walked away down the alley.

I wrapped, bundled and labeled those papers for two months. One night, the alternator on the delivery truck went out, and the headlights completely shut down. I coasted that truck down Highway 15 north into Wayne, the radio dead, no more music inside the cab. That was the last time I wrote an article for the city of "Wayne, America."

Willing and Ready

1870 – 1933. Floyd R. Knipplemeyer, Farmer.
Will concluded on said date of December 13th 1930, Cedar County,
Nebraska:

To son Floyd Jr.,
80 acres of broke ground of his choosing—quarter
horses and the 30 aught 6. East side of house.
All out buildings.

Son Ronald T.
87 Head of Angus.
West side of house. North forty.
Outhouse squatting rights.

Daughter Florence.
1 Hereford Bull.
Mother's wedding ring to do with as you choose.
All household appliances, furniture and accessories except, Ronald
T. and Floyd Junior's beds, kitchen table and wood stove.
Said savings of $16,328 and 33 cents.

Neighbor.
Floyd Sr. grants permission to finally move fence at the
south end of Snake Creek.
You're welcome you son of a bitch.

Witness. Mary A. Armkanecht. Dec. 13th 1933.

MIDWEST BUMPER STICKERS

A Retrospective II.

Nobody Knows I'm a Lesbian

Talk DERBY to ME

Life was easier when boys had cooties

I Love
My Wife

Dance Dad

Keep Your Dick Beaters OFF My Escort

Boobies make me smile

Driver picks the music. Shotgun shuts his cakehole.
Oh you think Peterbilt is overpriced so is your wife.

I'd rather be hang gliding

I'm A Hot Tubber

I'd rather be
riding her, too

I'd rather be CUMMIN than GOING

Save the *Ta Tas*

If it has tires or tits, it's trouble

Get the HELL Outta the WAY, Grannie's late for BINGO

Native
Thunder Clan

Red Hair, Don't Care

BEWARE THE MARE!
                    BACK OFF, City Boy

Silly boys, Jeeps are for girls

I LOVE CONNIE

Somewhere in Texas, There's a Village Missing an Idiot

If You Think My Truck is Smokin',
You Should See My Wife

I Like it Dirty
        I Like 'em Dropped
                Let's Do It

                        If you're gonna ride my bumper
                        you'd better put a saddle on it!

        DON'T LAUGH MISTER. YOUR DAUGHTER COULD BE
                        ON BOARD!

Retired HOOTERS GIRL

            You Just Got Passed by a Girl
            (same car) *Bite Me*
            (same car) If You Are Going to Ride My Ass At Least
                                Pull My Hair

BAD ASS TOYZ AREN'T JUST FOR BOYZ

My Other Car is a BROOM (viewed West River)

            No one cares about your stick figure family

Diesel Fumes Make Me Horny

Bone Chalk

My father-in-law wakes from a night's rest and pulls his socks up high to his knees, pulls his v-neck tee-shirt down over his belly, grabs the overalls that are hanging on the cast-iron heater and puts them on, both legs at a time. This is how I imagine it. I can hear him now, rustling with his boots. He grabs his hat and fists the bill. He gathers his thoughts and carries himself downstairs to the kitchen where I join him. He turns on the AM Philco Deluxe Cathedral to 570 WNAX out of Yankton, South Dakota. The announcer is talking humidity and heat—a scorcher of a day.

Sunny skies and dry. Another barnburner.

Jack doesn't find this amusing. He's German, a third generation farmer whose life depends on this land. Common sense matters to Jack. Family matters. The colt in the barn matters. A good pair of overalls and the little blip of a town that some people call Hardlyanything, Nebraska, where he's from, matters. When there isn't any rain and hasn't been any rain in weeks, it's no laughing matter. He plays with the radio's dial—trying to find another station, but the reception here is weak.

It's time for the Five State Trader. We have someone on line one. You looking for something today or are you selling?

This is Floyd from Viborg.

Well, hello, Floyd. You buying or selling?

I said, this is Floyd from Viborg.

Floyd, I'm going to have to ask you to turn down the volume of your radio. You're feeding back.

Oh. Right.

Go ahead now, Floyd.
I've got some tin for sale.
Okay.
Have about a hundred sheets. They're about one foot by three foot.
Sounds like you've been tearing down an outbuilding, Floyd.
Yes, I have. Building just buckled at the knees.
And how much would you like for the tin?
I'd like to get about a buck a sheet.
Okay. And how can listeners get a hold of you?
I already told you, this is Floyd, from Viborg.
A phone number, Floyd, we need a phone number.

I watch Jack pace in the kitchen, the Formica table, dishes in the sink and toaster looking on. He sits down at the kitchen table and deals himself a game of solitaire. His hands are calloused and scarred from years of hard work, the red ink of the cards smeared and dull.

The game, set up to win, has beaten him. He gathers the cards and puts the deck in the front pocket of his bib overalls. I sit down. He hands me an apple. He starts chewing on one, too. "Go on," he says. So, I take a bite. "You won't believe this," he continues, "but I was at the dump yesterday and I found this perfectly good bag of apples just sitting there. And now we're eating them." He smiles. Continues to chew.

He makes his way out the front door, which is always unlocked. He walks down the narrow lane about a hundred feet and looks into the rising sky. He turns and turns, trying to spot any sign of clouds. He takes to one knee, hunkering down to see under the old oak—to make sure he hasn't missed something off on the far horizon.

"Well. Let's go to town," he says.

We climb into his '76 Chevy pickup. One of the wooden barns leans into a dying cedar tree where Jack keeps some of his machinery. The foundation of the decaying barn is trapped by weeds that seem to form a barrier around it. One of the sliding doors is off its roller and slumps open. A disc is parked inside and what is left of the wagon Jack's team of workhorses used to pull. I don't know if it's the fumes from inside the cab of the truck or the heat, but sometimes if I stare too long into the darkness of that barn, I can see shadows of men hunched over in the back of that wagon. He was the last farmer in Cedar County to use a team of draft horses to sow oats. He never had a well dug so he could install a center-pivot on his land. If rain was sufficient for the year, the crop was good.

In a sienna-colored picture I will take of him and hang in our house, Jack is standing inside a different barn on his farm—rope in hand. There's a metal trough tipped on its side. He has most of his back to the camera. The cedar posts lean with his not-so-sturdy frame. He has lost weight in the picture, his belt cinched more to keep his jeans pulled up. The picture captures him in that barn for the last time—a month before he would leave the farm and move to town for good.

Now, though, the garage and a few outbuildings still have life in them. The roofs are tin. Hell, everything is tin nowadays. It's easier to burn the barn and build a metal machine shed than fix it up. There are two livestock barns out in the pasture with their original stone foundations. It's a shame to see any of this fall. To the south of us, it's soybeans in weedless rows. To the north—field corn struggling to grow. Sam, the blue heeler, runs alongside the truck. "You know," Jack says, "that dog would follow us all the way to town if I'd let him. Go home. Git," he hollers, and Sam stops and turns back home.

When we get to the end of the lane, we stop. We are waiting for anyone, anyone at all, to come by, and finally, Floyd Knipplemeyer, the neighbor from down the road, slowly creeps around the bend and heads our direction. Jack guns the accelerator out of his lane until we are in the middle of the road and then turns so we are hood to hood with Floyd's approaching truck. "This will slow him down," he says.

Jack hangs his arm out the window, as if to ask or gesture a concern. The neighbor stops. We are in the middle of the road—I guess he doesn't have a choice. We pull over to our side and up to his cab window.

"Well, hello, Jack. What can I do you for?"

"Call for rain?"

"Boy. We could use ourselves some rain. Some rain would be good. But today. Not so sure, Jack, not so sure."

"Well." Jack takes the feed cap from his head, studying it for any sure sign; his face is weathered, his chiseled chin is stubbled—the top of his forehead a lot whiter than the deep brown of his face and neck. "I reckon there's a chance."

"Heh. I reckon. There's always a chance." Floyd looks up to the ceiling of his cab, his eyes a flurry of impatience and then hits the side of his pick-up with his left hand, pushes on the accelerator to make a point, puts the single tree back in gear and then continues on his way.

What possesses a man to move to the middle of the country—to an unpopulated region to work for himself? Granted, Jack was born and raised here. He never left. It's what he knows. There's something to be said about solitude and working for yourself. There's also something to be said about waiting for quite a while at the end of the lane for someone—anyone—to drive by and then abruptly pulling out in front of them just to talk. I wouldn't be able to do it for long. I need to be around people. I like anticipating the unexpected. I need constant interaction—pleasant and unpleasant—with complete strangers, in fact. It baffles me to wonder what working forty-plus years on your own in relative isolation does to a man. Where's the place a man goes to really say what's on his mind? And to whom? To town? To the bar? To confession? These are the questions that continue to interest me when I look at this man.

Material goods are of little importance to Jack. He's a guy who buys his youngest daughter two new tires instead of four. I'll never forget one of the first birthdays I traveled to the farm with Linda, my girlfriend at the time. He'd left her birthday present out in the garage. She saw the two tires and was very happy. Like the spoiled, naïve city kid I was, I asked, "Where are the other two?"

She said, "I don't need four tires. I need two."

It would become very clear to me, very quickly, that Linda understood her father's world. What he was up against—the struggles to raise and provide for a large family at a time when so many farms were being taken over by large conglomerates. I would argue that Jack tried in his own way to know his children's worlds however he could while maintaining the daily and oftentimes never-ending chores of running the home place. The author Kent Meyers writes in his memoir *The Witness of Combines:*

> I know my own children as well as I do because I enter their worlds. I play games with them, read their books, talk about their lives, go to their soccer games. As they grow older, however, I struggle to find ways to let them enter my world, a thing my father did so easily and naturally with his children— though we often grumbled about it.
>
> The shelves of parenting sections of bookstores are filled with titles telling modern parents how to know their children, how to interpret their moods and signals. My father, I think, was not so concerned with that. He was more concerned with his children knowing him.
>
> I don't believe in a "work ethic"—that work

equates with goodness. Yet I'm quite sure that when work is performed by parents and children together toward a necessary and ultimately moral good—for instance, so that animals don't starve, or so that a family can make a living and stay together—it serves to pass on the story and meaning of parents' lives more effectively than anything else.

I once made the mistake of tailgating a guy in a pickup on the highway into town. He wasn't going fast enough for me so I said what I routinely said at that time, "Go back to the farm." And when those words left my lips, Linda looked at me very serenely and said, "Don't ever say that again."

Perhaps an attitude like mine back then comes from jealousy, really; maybe that's the thing city kids never admit to, that we're all just a little resentful we never had to learn some of the things that were so crucial to survival for some families. Not many of us will admit it; rather, we might make fun of some unkempt, country-boy bumpkins. But if I am honest with myself, that's what always astonished me about the rural way of life—how it taught something I knew I never had. I hung out with city kids who might know how to change oil in a car, clean a carburetor (maybe), or put a nail in the wall, but we never had to be relied on to do something for the good of the family. We simply picked up the phone and called a repair man if our fathers couldn't get the job done. And as I continued to beat around rural areas, nicknames like city-slicker didn't bother me a bit—I had a hunger to learn and an appetite for this life and culture.

I remember once again driving around with Linda, looking at her neighbor's farms. Every mile or two, a new cluster of trees would appear, and at the end of a long gravel driveway there'd be another big mailbox with the same last name written on it. I looked over at Linda and said, "You have a very big family. I bet your family reunions are a blast." She looked over at me and didn't say a word at first. Then, as we continued to drive, I said it again, "There's another one."

She spoke up. "We might all be distantly related, but we don't have family reunions." It would take me another few years to figure out what she meant by that and to understand the dynamics of such a loaded sentence.

And, in time, I also learned the difference between needs and wants. One of my fondest memories of Jack is him standing out in a field of oats. We were standing in a spot which allowed a guy to see for miles around entire sections of land. At that time, I could vaguely calculate what section was his and what might be his neighbors'. As we stood there in silence, he said to me, "Listen to that." And I did. I could hear the knee-high oats brushing together, whispering. It was very peaceful. *How many souls make up the inexhaustible winds? / How many of them taught with their bones' chalk?* Wrote Don Welch in his poem, "Requiem for a Teacher."

After a good minute, he said, "Look at this. Maybe someday you might like to farm something like this, too." And I was eager to farm. The grass did look greener. I was eager to learn all there was to learn about rural living.

Common sense values were principles I was embracing. I admired this agrarian way of life—the romance of working for yourself—the seclusion and privacy, as long as there was gas in the Chevy to get to town. The silence of a game of solitaire, or the stillness of a serious game of euchre after a day in the field—all of it was appealing. It was a quiet competition I'd imagined that I had never experienced.

I'd like to believe I began to start truly listening then, too. I always run my mouth. Maybe because as an only child it makes me feel less alone. But here, out in the great wide open, I can watch this man—study his characteristics. A lot of the family has this quick wit and humor about them. It's hilarious, but you have to be paying attention to see and hear it. Linda and her father have this genuine eagerness in their voices—and also, a tone of sincere curiosity and interest whether they truly understand what I'm talking about or not. Oftentimes, they might not even care. But they listen.

After dinner we often come up for air, push our chairs away from the table, and listen to Jack tell stories. There isn't anything else to do. I am learning a lot about delivery—when to interject and try to up the ante.

Jack and I are heading north to Fordyce—to town. Fordyce lies on eighty acres and is south of Yankton, South Dakota about twelve miles, along highway 81. This is where the local freebee gas station koozie reads: *We wish for World Peace or any Piece*. It's also a place that distributes County License Plate Directories. If you see a car somewhere, you can just look up the last four digits of the plate to see whose it is.

The gravel rumbles underneath the bed of the truck. Jack's speed increases at the crest of each new hill. Sometimes I worry that he may doze off, but he never has. We lose traction in the loose gravel, and I tense up. He pulls us away from the ditch. He never says much, and I think that's what bothers me the most. We can be hell-bent for a culvert, and he'll still be gazing ahead, fixed on whatever it is he fixes on.

Fordyce is a small town that acts as a watering hole, gas station, lumber yard, and place to store grain, for those who need it. The Co-Op is one of the only things that has survived here. There's a butcher shop that has changed ownership a few times, but it has survived. At the "mall," a building that holds the convenience store, gas station and mechanic, there's a sign that reads: *Too Small For A Town Drunk, So We Take Turns.*

The Bar and Grill is hit and miss every few years. There's St. John the Baptist Catholic Church. There's the bank, which was robbed a few years ago. They never did catch the guy. It's always a guy, isn't it?

A lot has changed over the years since this town was booming—all 192 people. According to the only history book about the area, the bank and saloon were the first businesses to rise in 1907. When the town was rolling, there were two grocery stores, a post office, a meat market, a pool hall, a drug store, lumberyard, blacksmith shop, train depot, café, gas station and feed store. It's hard to imagine that now. Many of the buildings here are as empty as the old barns on Jack's farm and almost as decayed.

Jack creeps along at a snail's pace when we reach town. I try to spot someone in the newspaper-covered storefront windows. Just a glimpse or shadow. There are two pickups on the main street that runs through town. A dog relieves himself on the corner of another abandoned building. It's July, and a Christmas decoration, a snowman with a rather large corncob pipe, still hangs on a lamppost. Jack stops the truck. Kills the engine. I can hear someone drop a tire iron from the other side of town. The truck engine ticks. Someone coughs somewhere.

"The great escape happened here during the Depression years. Have I told you about the great escape?" Jack asks, chuckling to himself. "They were having free shows in town. There was a pool hall and watering hole a guy might visit from time to time. There in the center of town was this flagpole by the bar and picture house—right there in the middle of Main Street." I glance out the window of the truck, looking for the pole, but I don't see anything.

"We were with Gunner Lammers, who was driving a '37 Chevy. He was an ornery guy. He kept driving around and around that flagpole, and the streets were crowded yet, and he was spitting gravel up everywhere, into a lot of the stores. They hadn't paved the roads yet, you know." Jack pauses to chuckle.

This is what I love about my father-in-law. A guy could learn more about the history of Nebraska by tagging along with him than he could in any book. When Jack gets to telling one of his stories, they are slow and carefully delivered. When he's in the mood, it's magical. To get anything from people around here is like pulling teeth. I rest my arm on the windowsill of the truck.

"See now, the night cop in town didn't even have a car at that time. He walked. Gunner finally got tired of tearing around that flagpole, and we pulled up to the curb and went in to old man Poeggler's pool hall. Gunner left the keys in the car. A lot of folks did that back then. We come back out a while later, and those keys were gone. Gunner starts pissing and moaning and shouting into the street at no one. Soon enough, here comes the night cop. He came and handcuffed Gunner for disorderly conduct. Said he was tired of kids ripping around that flagpole. He gave us the keys and told us to get home.

"Sth." Is the sound he makes as he leans back in the driver's seat and looks up and out the corner of one eye—checking to see if I'm paying attention.

"So, we all figured we needed to do something. Hell, we needed a ride home. The jail was right over there on Main Street." He points without moving his hand from the steering wheel.

"So we walked north on Omaha Street there after about an hour and walked down to the jailhouse. We went in to talk to Gunner. He's the only one there in this steel cage—night cop gone on the beat again. And he said, 'Hell, you know, this cage don't run all the way clear to the ceiling. Three of you guys,' he said, 'could lift that up, so I could get out underneath, you know.'" Jack started laughing and scratching his forearm. "Only thing was that we weren't sure we could keep it lifted long enough. We didn't want him to get under there for us to let it down and kill him. But, we needed that ride— couldn't just take the guy's car without him.

"We got a hold of that cage and tried it a bit and we got it and lifted it up. He was a free man. That cage was a heavy sonofabitch. We were all out the door in no time. Night cop was out somewhere with his nightstick—we fixed his wagon. Hah! And so it went. We left town. Nobody got hurt."

Jack starts the truck, drives a block to the edge of town, turns back onto the gravel road, and we head south, peering again into the open road.

Fortnite vs. W.C. Franks
Millard Plaza, Circa 1980's

I'm explaining what an arcade is to my daughter, or trying to while she plays Fortnite, a shoot 'em up apocalyptic game. In Fortnite, she gains rewards through modern-day missions to advance her characters and support her team. When she's on a roll, she racks up an arsenal of some pretty bad-ass weapons which make it possible to maneuver and conquer more difficult terrain.

"I just killed two people on Fortnite."

"Great!" her mother responds.

"I'm a no skin who killed a guy who has skin. I was like, dude, he was shooting me and I shot him then he was dead."

"You know that's not right?" I interrupt.

"Yes. But, I'm a terrible aim, anyway."

"What do you mean you don't have any skin?"

"Come here and look." She points to the screen. Her character is a fit female with desert camo on. Looks pretty normal, besides the huge ax in her hand.

"I'm a default character which means you don't buy skins. See those guys? They bought that costume." She and a group of her teammates aggressively start hacking at the overturned Hummer.

"You know what, I'm not sure what's in here. Why are we hacking at this thing with axes, people? Maybe there's a chest or something in there. Forget this. I'm just going to kill people," she says.

"You are kinda running right down the middle of the battlefield, aren't ya?" I warn her. I mean she is only ten years old. She has to watch out for herself.

"Yeah. But I need more mushrooms."

I interrupt her playing and tell her my generation invented video games. Which we kinda did. Atari released Pong the year I was born—1972. In October 1958, Physicist William Higinbotham created what is thought to be the first video game. It was a very simple tennis game, similar to the classic 1970s video game, Pong, and it was quite a hit at a Brookhaven National Laboratory open house.[12]

Atari was great if you could afford one, which none of us could. I waited ten years until the Atari 5200 came out. That year was revolutionary in the Reese household. Once I was old enough to venture out on my own, my friends and I hung out at arcades. I'm flashing back to W.C. Franks in Millard, Nebraska. Or the Western Bowl, which is still there. Here we learned to wait patiently while some snot-nosed kid lined the bottom of the machine's screen with quarters, which basically reserved his spot for the whole afternoon. That meant his Mom gave him his whole allowance. Sometimes we'd accidentally unplug the machine to wreck his high score and to ground him in the reality that there were other people living in this world who had two or three quarters collectively that they had managed to find in seat cushions and wanted to play, too.

MIDWEST BUMPER STICKERS
A Retrospective III.

DRIVE IT Like You STOLE IT

Underwood 2016
Don't Mess with My Country

SHIT better not HAPPEN

American as FUCK

Stop Honking I'm Masturbating

USPS Go POSTAL

Chuck Norris Forecast Cloudy
with a 90% Chance of Pain

Think about honking if you like conceptual art

I'd Rather Be at a
Neil Diamond Concert

Against abortion?
Don't have one.

The only Coke I do is Diet

Stop the TransCanada Pipeline

Fact of Life even after Tuesday a Calendar says WTF

I know Jack Shit

I **AM NOT** a LIBERAL
Cartel (same car)
26.2
13.1   HALF MY HEART IS IN Iraq
0.0

You can't be both Catholic and pro-choice
(Same car) **I'm Catholic and I vote**

Hearing voices in your head?
Turn OFF Fox News

EXTREME Republican

WWII I served
War is Not the Answer (same car)

Republican....
because not everyone can be on welfare!

I REMEMBER KOREA

Gayville Fire and Rescue

Honk if parts fall off

If the Fetus You Save is Gay,
Will You Still Fight for Its Rights?

STURGIS Ride To Live

Will Brake for Explosives!!!

Socialism Sucks

Next time you are perfect try walking on water.

Water Boarding is for Pussies
Green Bay **Fudge** Packers

Eat More Kale

**IF YOU CAN'T STAND BEHIND OUR TROOPS,
FEEL FREE TO STAND IN FRONT OF THEM**

SAVE the Boobies

COWBOYS FOR CHRIST

I MISS President Reagan

My other tractor is my neighbor's
It's not the destination, it's the journey

My kid defends freedom for your honor student

Ain't Nothing Meaner than a Marine,
'Cept his Mamma

Angry. Need a Weapon. Pray Rosary.

I'm not tailgating, I'm drafting

GET OFF YOUR PHONE AND DRIVE

Horn Not Working Watch For Finger

Working for an **Idiot Free** America

You are in INDIAN COUNTRY

REPUBLICAN WOMEN
are the life of the party

Where the Heck is WALL DRUG

Siouxland Eye Bank Please Donate

You Can Have My Book
When You Pry It from My Cold Dead Hands

SUPPORT OUR TROOPS BRING THEM HOME

Cowboy UP

Sure You Can Trust the Government Just Ask an Indian

It's Bush's Fault
(viewed in Marshall, MN; close enough)

**Near As I Can Tell
We're Somewhere Behind Mt. Rushmore**

Buckets, Indians and Habaneros

Back in 2000, my friend Carl, who still calls me bucket calf, told me the only way to write about something was to go out and do it yourself. "Besides, I'm getting tired of you following me around." And to be honest, I was tired of some writers I was seeing on occasion in academic hallways trying to portray a romantic way of life on the Great Plains while they sat behind their comfy desks—"pencil pushers," like I'd been called more than once. I did need to get dirty; do some "real" work.

I looked the part sometimes. Hung out with horse-breakers. I bragged about roping calves from atop a stallion because I'd done it twice (in a small corral). I was the only guy in the English department who had. And if I was studying to be a professor, well, I still had work to do. Otherwise my students who grew up on a farm or ranch would see right through me. I knew a guy could be a thinker and a do-er. And I knew from failure you could try everything until they kicked you out. In *The Lost Notebooks of Loren Eiseley*, Eiseley said:

> The uses of a great professor are only partly to give us knowledge; his real purpose is to take his students beyond knowledge into the transcendental domain of the unknown, the future and the dream—to expand the limits of the human consciousness… He must teach men not alone to dream, but to dream so substantially that they will never in after years capitulate through weakness to the demands of a passing and ephemeral materialism. It is in the nature of man to transcend himself. All teaching which

neglects this aspect of humanity will end in failure.
It will fail sooner or later because it constitutes a
denial, in fact a deprivation, of human nature.

I had to start burning my own inimitable brand for myself and
for my students. I became hell bent on gaining new experiences. I
was a firm believer in gonzo journalism and immersion—give me
the reins and let me buck it out. So I took Carl's advice and went to
work on a farm outside of town. No Experience Necessary. I fit.

Brant and his father farm a few hundred acres of corn and
beans—milk sixty head of Holstein. Brant, like his father, has a
high-pitched voice; at any given time, you might hear one of them
yelling out. It's a combination cry and the squeal of a stuck pig—
"Ahhruugghheeeee!" And they do this for no apparent reason,
except to hear themselves.

Brant's worked hard his whole life, and from what I can gather,
he seems to enjoy it. He could be one of the nicest guys I've met.
His suspenders hold his work shirt in place and his pants up. The
man genuinely loves good hats, Keystone Light beer, and the
Cleveland Indians. He is a guy who frequently cracks himself up.
"Pick that little weed, pick that little weed," he'll say, when he sees
any female bend over. This, he believes, is one of his funnier jokes.

Over probably too many beers, Brant agreed to let me be his
hired hand for the summer. I had never worked on a farm, and
besides the early hours, which I had trouble keeping, the $5.50
an hour seemed fair enough. I was a grad student at the time and
needed work until my fall teaching assistantship kicked in.

For my initiation, I scoop cow shit until it forms a ravine, and
the piss and manure flow downhill from where the Holsteins stand
and chew. After I pass the test, Brant and I go to Tractor Supply
Company, and he buys me my first pair of Tingley work boots. I still
haven't thrown them out.

The second week at the place and I haven't planted a damn thing.
I had envisioned myself behind a tractor or a combine, plowing and
planting, but I'm stuck up on Brant's garage tearing off old shingles
that will soon be replaced with tin. Everything is turning to tin now
on farms. I suppose it's easier to burn the barn and build a machine
shed than fix most things up. It's a shame. The craftsmanship that
went in to many first homesteads is long gone. How on earth can a
guy afford to scrape and paint barns and outbuildings on a regular
basis when crop prices stay consistently low? Government subsidies
and mailbox loans are how most remaining family farmers in this area
stay afloat. That and second and sometimes third jobs around the
clock.

Brant has a picture hanging in his kitchen of what this place used to look like. It's an aerial shot. I can see his father waving to the cameraman in the plane. The whole place is green and fresh. The buildings glisten, and nothing seems out of order or overgrown. It was beautiful. It was truly something.

Stepping outside of Brant's modest two-story home, I see three dilapidated outbuildings for calves and hogs and a machine shed/apartment, which serves as his father's napping quarters. There's a fully functioning milk barn and two large silos—"his and her tombstones," Brant jokes, marking the farm's decline.

There are weevils everywhere—relentless little bugs that find their way into all of my body's crevices. They are infesting the grain here. It's really hot. I've never been in the sun this long in my life. The weather gauge often reads over 100 degrees. Try standing in 100-degree sunlight for hours. Try laying irrigation pipe in 110 degree weather with no breeze—you'll likely run to the pickup, drive to the home place (if you can make it that far to find a toilet) to find relief. Otherwise, you'll dump there in the field. Even when you've drunk gallons of water, the dehydration still wears you down.

The gravel roads around the home place are littered with aluminum beer cans. Brant tells me we'll pick these cans up when it slows down and make more per bushel recycling than he will on corn. I'm here with dirt, dry wind, and a sorry-ass dog who has been hit by a pickup too many times. I would be overwhelmed if this were my own place. There's too much to do for Brant and his aging father, and a lot of days, I'm not sure I make a dent.

The closest thing I've seen to farming these first weeks are the Holsteins in the field at night; the bucket calves I feed in the afternoon; a hog I throw scraps to after lunch; and the bucket of this old John Deere 3020 I am throwing shingles into.

They won't give me rein to buck out this tractor. When the loader bucket is full, I have to inch off the roof and walk out into the beans to flag one of them down. Waste of time, I think, and 98 degrees is too damn hot to be walking in any field so they can come and dump the shingles on the burn pile themselves.

After watching Brant dump the thing a few times, I figure it can't be too hard to run this rig. Call me a greenhorn, call me whatever you like, but I came here to drive a tractor. I'm a city kid, no doubt. But I can drive. The only problem is it's old like the rest of the stuff here—the gearshift directions are gone from rain and rust. What I figure though, is reverse is back and drive is forward—simple enough. They'll know I'm driving the tractor soon enough, too—black cloud'll be pouring out of this erect muffler. I'll just let off this clutch and be on my way.

I wait half an hour before I walk a line of beans to tell them their tractor has gone awry. I phone my wife twice, leaving paranoid messages on our answering machine. "The goddamn tractor hit the garage. This isn't good. The gears are all backwards and shit. And I couldn't put the thing in reverse. It went the wrong way and it's all my fault."

No one picks up when I call home for counseling. I'm in Brant's house sweating profusely. Just tell him the truth, I keep saying to myself.

I'm working for peanuts here, but the thought of letting Brant down, especially this early on, dismays me. I should have listened to him. I know how to work. Doing this gives me a sense of belonging to something bigger. I'm not just some waiter or telemarketer; what I am doing this summer serves a purpose. I'm finding out what Eiseley's transcending human nature looks like—a tractor with a loader bucket embedded into a garage. And, with all this schooling, I should know better. I have two degrees. I'm working on a third—a Ph.D. for Christ's sake—I'm going to be a doctor. Not one that can feel and heal you, but I don't want my lack of experience to show.

I spot Brant out in the beans. He's on a tractor. The beans are coming in strong. As I walk out to flag him down, I stop occasionally to pull up a weed. Maybe he'll see me do this, praise me for thinking and taking charge before the beans become infested. By the time I make it out to him, I'm drenched. I can see his father standing next to a nearby tractor—I hear him squeal, "Aagghhhruuughheee?"

In my head I keep replaying the episode—starting the tractor, turning around to look behind me, inching off the clutch, and the loud smash and crash of a fuel tank I ran straight into. The tractor moving in the wrong direction. My head and body jerking the wrong way. The frame of the roof lifting up and then smacking down on the walls of the garage. I see it again and again. The loader bucket lifting the side of the roof completely up and off the garage's existing frame. I can see myself reaching for the key in the ignition and turning it off. I take my foot off the brake and watch as the roof crashes back down onto the frame of the garage. I see the fuel tank on its side. I can see myself standing on the brakes— dumbfounded and speechless. How did I get to be such an idiot? Jesus, I'm in graduate school. They don't just let anyone in.

"What happened?" Brant hollers at me. "Looks like you just seen a ghost."

"I drove the loader bucket into the side of the garage," I tell him. "It's still standing—I think it will be okay." Brant doesn't say anything. He just stares at me. Then he turns away to look at something—anything, I imagine, other than the sight of me.

"Did you hit anything else?" he asks.

"A fuel tank."

"Goddamn—which one?" He raises his voice. "What color was it?"

"The red one. The rusted-looking one."

"All right, then. Stay off the tractor. I'll be in after a while to check it out."

I want to tell Brant to come now. Fire me now if you're going to do it. But I don't want to press my luck. I feel like I'm in high school again—staying after school for something stupid that I did. All I can think to do is walk away and continue to pick weeds as I come upon them. I can't climb up on the roof to finish the job and, by the time I reach the end of the row, I want to give up, call it quits, go home, and lick my wounds.

Brant finds me feeding the hog. I look up to take my medicine.

"You know, you're lucky you didn't hit the white fuel tank. It's full, and that could have been a problem. Stay off the tractor."

"Okay."

"You play with fire, Jimbo, and you will get burned," Brant says. "You know, the old man has been doing this for how many years—forty or more, and he just drove the combine into the side of the milk barn last week. Not sure if he fell asleep or what. Shit happens. I'm glad you didn't hit my truck. That would have made me unhappy."

In the afternoon, Brant and I fill five feeder buckets full of oats and drive them out to an adjacent field. He grabs a couple of beers from the cooler and hands me one. I don't think I'm going to get fired. And this Keystone Light is the best beer I've ever had.

I walk the buckets out, two at a time, and fill the empty troughs. I stand back. The cows see me and start to beller. I pick out a spot on the old oak to count the blue-black and white as they trot up the hill to feed. Today, I'm one head short. Brant counts, and he's short one, too. We drive the pickup over to the south creek. And there, like a gopher in soft dirt, stuck knee-deep in quicksand, is the last of this breed.

"Son-of-a-bitch!" Brant hollers. He slams the single tree in park and is out of the truck in no time. I jump out and follow him. He shimmies down the bank of the creek, trying not to fall face first down the embankment. "Stay up there," he hollers to me. "You'll scare the cow." The Hereford is bellering. It sounds like a worn-out transmission—a driver who can't keep his foot from tapping the accelerator. A repetitive on-again-off-again noise that doesn't stop the whole time Brant assesses the situation.

"There's a rope in the pickup," he hollers to me, "behind the driver's seat. Get it and bring it here."

I grab the rope and throw it down to him. He readjusts the loop at one end and tosses it towards the cow. The Hereford's head is swimming towards the sky; and the third time Brant throws, he gets the loop around it. Brant braces himself as best he can in the creek's bank and mud beneath him, and pulls. The cow is at least twice his size and doesn't budge. At the bank of the creek, he is at a tug-of-war with the animal. The cow's legs are almost completely immersed in mud. Brant looks like he might pull the cow's neck clean off.

"This isn't going to work," he tells me. "Go back to the place and get the tractor and drive it out here. There's a log chain in the garage, if it hasn't fallen down yet. Bring that, too."

I haul ass in the pickup across the section and find the tractor exactly where I left it. The garage has not fallen down, and there, hanging on one of its walls amongst the clutter, are long ropes of chain. I grab the ropes, one at a time, and pull them towards the loader bucket. They are heavy. When I'm on the tractor, I don't spend a lot of time thinking. I'm clear of danger and turn it over and play with the gears until I'm sure I've figured out which lever controls the bucket and which puts the thing in gear. I lower the bucket and kill the engine. Get out and load the chain. Luckily, the thing turns over again, and I'm off, knocking the throttle into high, burning down the dirt road, thinking, yes, I do have a purpose here. And, shortly, after Brant wraps circles of chain around the back of the Hereford's front legs and belly, he pulls the cow free with the help of the tractor.

* * *

As the summer of my farming apprenticeship progresses, I am demoted to "Official Barn Tearer Downer." Basically, Brant doesn't know what else to do with me between chores, laying pipe and fixing fence. He doesn't really trust me behind the wheel of a tractor, and I refuse to pull any more weeds from the bean field unless he pays me as much as the high school kids get, which is $3.00 more than the $5.50 I agreed to. So between laying pipe in the morning and early afternoon and doing evening chores, I'm stuck here, at the renter's half-acre spread, tearing down this old wooden barn.

Most of the barn has given way to gravity and wind. "The

barn just buckled at the knees," Brant says. To me, it looks like it is praying or dying, or praying that it won't die.

The barn is old and gray. Red hues still linger on a few of the boards I pull from the south side, but the rest of the paint is worn or gone altogether. Brant says I can keep anything I find inside the barn, which has me a little motivated. I already found this old SuperSweet feed sign buried under one of the 2x8's. Most of the orange paint is still on the sign. I also found the blades of half a windmill. Where the other half is, I don't know. My hope is that I'll find it when this mess is cleaned up.

The renters have a nice spread—a small, two-bedroom white ranch house with a detached garage. There's an underground cellar for their canned goods, which is between the garage and house. Their yard is green fescue. Their lane is clean and mowed to the gravel. They have an enormous garden—it's bigger than their house. Rows of beans, a variety of peppers, squash, sweet corn, tomatoes and peas. They have an adjacent garden strictly for asparagus. The mulch between the rows of vegetables is carefully placed—not too close to the stalks of the plants. Everything seems in order except this barn. And the renters started complaining to Brant about it. That's why I'm here. To tear it down and make room for another enormous garden for these people who don't pay more than $300 a month rent and who, to my very eyes, don't move an inch to help out when a few cows get out on their place.

I asked Brant's mother a week ago if she'd consider renting the house to someone new—someone like me and my wife. I even agreed to help with the milking every other weekend. Told her once I learned, I could even hook the suckers up myself. She said, "No. Besides, they pay on time."

Give me a break. The renters are a waste of space. All Brant's mother does is complain about milking. If she can't see the beauty in this deal, well, to hell with it. I don't want the place that bad. But I truly had started fooling myself that I was finding my calling. I might not know what a JD 3020 was but, like anything else, I was asking and learning from my mistakes. I was failing miserably a lot of the time, but I was okay with it. I would not deprive myself of this opportunity of immersion.

Once, I asked the renter if he could spare a few stalks of asparagus. He said no. He's got a 12 x 20-foot plot of asparagus and said no. I was dumbfounded. I'd been tearing down this enormous barn at the place he lived, and he was downright rude. He rarely waved or said hello. Out here in this section of land off the highway, it seems like we are on our own island. When someone doesn't say hi, it's troubling. So every time the tight-sphincter leaves after lunch, I wave to him, smile, then go fill a feeder bucket full of asparagus and steal a few tomatoes.

The only thing good about this place is George. At least that's what we call him. Brant's father started calling him that and it stuck.

"Why does he call me George?" George asks.

"Because that's your name, isn't it?"

"No," he says. "But I like George."

So it stuck. George it is. He's quiet and peculiar. Brant says he's from a broken home. Doesn't know who his father is, and his mother ran off when he was too young to know better. Brant says these are his foster parents. The renters have legal custody is what I know.

I say George is peculiar because, well, because I never see him playing with other kids. There's no emotion. Just deadpan. He's probably eleven years old, from what I can guess. At eleven, I was gone. Free to roam. George doesn't do much roaming. He's got a weird kind of limp when he walks. The only pleasure he seems to get out of life is coming out here and helping me tear down this barn. He helps me hold the salvageable 2x8's on saw horses as I hammer out every last rusted nail from them. When we finish one, he'll smile, and carry the plank over to a stack of keepers we've started. Brant's daughter told me the kids make fun of George at school because he's so shy. Because he walks funny.

Almost every afternoon he's out here helping me. Then he'll be gone for days at a time. The curtains will be pulled at the renter's place—the sound of piano keys—redundant chord progressions and John Thompson techniques echo in the air. I stare at the house, and it looks like some sort of abandoned oasis. The heat radiates off the grass and gravel that separates me from the strange world that my mind sees inside that house. I'd like some ice to add to my water jug, but I know better than to go to their front door and ask. Brant told me they aren't very hospitable. The few brief encounters I've had with them out here in the middle of nowhere aren't pleasant. They never wave, which is bizarre. If you want to draw some attention to yourself in the country—don't wave. I've been out here long enough to learn that. In the city, it's practically a prerequisite to mind your own business, but out here, that doesn't work.

On these days, I always think it's wrong. Gorgeous summer afternoons—aside from the heat. George not around—cooped up, forced into some sort of homegrown recital. Playing the piano is for rainy days and the winter. Not July afternoons. If George is shy, fine. But let the kid come out and do something.

* * *

Brant and I are bored. I don't want to tear down the barn this afternoon, and he doesn't want to lay anymore "Arrrruuggheeee" irrigation pipe.

"Me neither," I say.

"Let's go screw with neighbor Al. Let's get some beer. I've got an idea."

Making $5.50 an hour and drinking beer is the best job I've ever had. Brant and I get a twelve pack of Keystone Light and drive a couple miles south to the neighbor's section. Al's place is kept up well. Al has an enormous machine shed behind his house where he hangs out most of the time. If you want to find him, he's usually in the field or in the machine shed listening to the radio. More likely, he's in the machine shed listening to a Cubs baseball game. With Sammy Sosa, Al has been regurgitating spittle through his teeth. He'll come over a six-pack strong, slurring his words, talking this and that about what the Cubs are going to do this year. I'm a Yankees fan, so, frankly, I don't give a rip what Al says. The odds are in my favor. The Yankees will likely make the playoffs, as will Brant's favorite team, the Indians, I believe.

We leave and drive back to Brant's place. "I want you to paint a big Cleveland Indian on Al's garage," Brant says. "Right in the middle—above the stalls. Come on, you're the writer, artist." We sit in his favorite plastic lawn chairs on his back porch, and we think about it. He leans back and laughs. "Manny Eats Sosa For Lunch!" He hollers. "I want you to paint that on there, too. Otherwise, you're fired."

I think about the proposition. $5.50 may not seem like much, but I do need the little bit of extra money until I go back to school and borrow more money from the government to finish my graduate degree.

"I'm pretty sure Al will shoot me if I paint that right on his garage. Especially if he's drunk enough," I tell Brant.

"Nahh. Al don't have no guns. Couldn't see straight to shoot them if he did."

"All right. But I'm not painting it on the garage. I've got a better idea."

We find an old cardboard refrigerator box—a big one. Now I know why these guys don't throw anything away. We break it down. Brant finds some of his daughter's paint and markers inside. He sits back in the lawn chair, throws me his baseball hat to refer to, and watches and corrects me as I draw my first, and likely last, Cleveland Indian.

"Not bad. Not bad," he comments. "Maybe after you're done with the barn, I'll have you paint that on the side of the silo."

I color the thing in—paint it the way Brant tells me—the feather red and the Indian's eyes looking off to the corner.

"That's good enough to hang in Jacob's Field," he tells me. "Hot damn!"

"Where's Jake's field at?" I ask. "I thought we were hanging this on Al's garage."

"Jacob's Field. In Cleveland, Jimbo. Get it straight."

Before I'm done, in big black bold letters I write Manny above the Indian. *Eats*—to the left of the Indian. Sosa—to the right. *FOR LUNCH!* In bold, below the Indian's head. Beautiful. Brant grabs a ladder, hammer, and nails. The painting, all laid out on cardboard, is really something. We pull back up to Al's place and honk a few times. He doesn't seem to be around. We get out. Brant climbs the ladder and holds the thing in place.

"Hold on to this thing so I don't fall. I think I'm getting drunk."

Brant hammers the first nail in. It's loud. Dangerously loud. But there's still no sign of Al. He continues with five more nails.

"That ain't going anywhere."

We get back to the truck and lay on the horn. Nothing. No one comes. We drink some more beer. Throw the empties in Al's lane. I can't believe we pissed away the whole day.

"Sure enough," Brant says after a while. "I'm drunk."

We take our supplies home and call it a day.

* * *

When I'm not here tearing down the barn, Brant has me painting his house. He's debating what he wants to do. His wife wants to get off the home-place and build new on another section of their land. She's sick of the Holsteins. The hogs. The weevils in her cereal and flour. The smell. I don't blame her. I try keeping their place clean, but then again, I'm the same guy that drove the tractor into the garage, so I don't have a lot of room to talk.

Brant says the more of the barn I tear down, the better the renter's place is looking to him. He says maybe they will relocate there. I'm all for it. Kick 'em out. They don't help out. Don't share. Keep George, I tell him. And I mean that. Whatever is going on in that house, it's weird. Besides picking weeds in their garden, harvesting lettuce and kale, I don't see them outside at all. Today, I caught George coming out of the underground cellar. I didn't see him go down there. His hands were full of canned goods. He didn't look up at me. The lady of the house stood on the front stoop and stared at me, then back at George. These people act like aliens from another planet. I waved again. She kept the door propped open for George to clear the threshold and then shut it. George kept saying no as he walked into the house. Up the lane, down the lane, to the cellar, to the house.

Later that afternoon, I walked down into the cellar. Brant had told me to stay out of their garden, to stay off their place. Maybe they saw me stealing asparagus, but Brant wasn't going to fire me for that. I could imagine him laughing at the renters, saying something like, aghh, it's just a few stalks of asparagus—perhaps reminding them I was tearing down this eyesore of a barn for them. But this was a little different. I was trespassing. The sun was blazing hot. I walked down the eight cellar steps that were lit up by one lone lightbulb. I assumed it would be dark. The lightbulb in the stairwell seemed odd. But George couldn't have turned it off. He had his hands full. The door at the bottom of the stairs was open. It didn't smell musty. It was dark inside, but I could see the shelves were painted white—all perfectly aligned with various jars of preserved vegetables. Jesus, it was a lot of food for three people. I just stood there on the bottom step, in the silence of the place and listened.

* * *

"Don't bring me down, Al! Don't bring me down, Al! Don't bring me down ow ow own, oh oh oh!" Brant sings from pickup cab to pickup cab on the road between both men's sections.

Two days after the Indian incident, Al is drinking Busch Light and looking particularly angry. It's hard to take him seriously.

"That's not how the song goes. It's Bruce, don't bring me down, Bruce!"

"Not the way I sing it. The struggle is real, Al."

"You wouldn't know anything about anyone nailing a Cleveland Indian to the top of my garage now, would ya'?"

"A Cleveland Indian. Well, a'll be. I thought you were a Cubs fan. Hey, Jimbo, you know anything about anyone nailing a Cleveland Indian to the top of Al's garage?"

"Nope."

"Some sorry sonofabitch thought it'd be funny to paint a picture, the same one you have on your hat there, on my garage."

"Is that so?" Brant says.

"Payback's a bitch," Al says and takes a long pull off his beer. All determined, like drinking the whole beer is going to prove something.

"Hey, Al, are you talking about the same Indian that had a slogan around his head. I think it says something like, Manny eats Sosa for dinner."

"*For lunch!* It says *Manny eats Sosa for lunch*. Not dinner. You do know who did it!" Al exclaims.

"Nope. Don't know anything about it." Brant belches. And we drive away.

* * *

I'm supposed to be tearing down the barn, but I can't find a pickup truck to drive over to the other section. Brant says to take his. But his truck isn't here. When I find it, I plan to drive holy hell out of it. I see two pickups. The starter doesn't work in the one. The other has a flat tire. I see a pickup bed full of tires. All of them flat.

I start walking. It's about one mile through the corn to the renter's place. It's three miles by gravel. The corn is too high, though. I have to take gravel. It is desolate out here. The highway is only a mile to the north from Brant's place. But here, a couple of miles south, I can't hear anything but the wind and my feet on dirt and rock. I can hear the gurgle of water occasionally coming from the pipe we laid last month. Gurgle. That may be all that's left. The farm pond is on its last puddle. We need rain. Over to my right is Al's spread. His center pivot isn't working again. On the end of his center-pivot hangs the largest pair of stained tightey-whities I've ever seen. That poor bastard. The neighbors around here are ruthless.

I hear the roar of a muffler coming. I recognize the truck. It's Brant's father's. Brant's driving. The truck stops.

"I left you a note. I told you you could take my rig," Brant says.

"I can't find it."

"Maybe the old man still has it. Get in."

"He's sleeping in the machine shed."

"What?"

We get back to the place. Brant looks around and starts kicking the dirt. "Well, where's my truck?" He goes in and yells at his father who doesn't know where his truck is either. "Al," Brant says. We get back into his father's beat-up pickup, the one where the driver's door doesn't shut, and we drive over to Al's place.

"Al, where's my truck?"

"You mean the navy blue 2000 Chevy extended cab with the Cleveland Indian logos in the back window? Don't know anything about it."

"Uh huh," Brant says under his breath. "We'll see." And we fish-tail out of Al's place; Brant, leaning outside the cab, grabs on to the driver's door for dear life. "He did something with it! I can feel it."

"Maybe your daughter took it," I offer.

"Yeah. Maybe."

We get back to the place and throw all the flat tires into the back of his dad's beat up S10. We drive and dump them off at a garage—nine tires in all. Every once in a while on the way back to the farm, I hear him cuss Al's name.

Ever since I drove the 3020 loader bucket into the garage, no one parks their car or truck in there. The garage door has been down and locked for almost two months. It's off limits until someone gets out here to take a look at it. Brant says he wants a professional to look it over. He doesn't want to park anything in it until then. I still haven't told him the whole roof came up and off the garage's existing frame, but he must suspect something.

We get back, and I glance over to the garage. It's not quite shut all the way.

"Hey. Look at that."

Brant jumps out of the S10 and raises the garage door. And there it is. Brant's navy blue 2000 Chevy extended cab with all the Cleveland Indian logos smiling back at him. Brant looks it over for any scratches—gets in and turns it over. He backs the thing up and parks it outside the garage. The cardboard Indian we nailed to Al's garage is in the bed of the truck.

"Sonofabitch," he says.

* * *

When I finished tearing down the barn, I returned to graduate school. I focused on my dissertation on the importance of rural aesthetics in contemporary American poetry and forgot about a lot of things that happened that summer, including George. I was reaching a part of my life where minimum-wage manual jobs would forever be behind me.

Two years later, standing in our rented house, staring at our tiny thirteen-inch television and the local news, I saw a picture of the renter's house, the two enormous gardens gone to weeds, and the television news reporter told me about the foster parents, accused of force-feeding him homegrown habanero peppers.

It took a moment to sink in. Then, the silence of the cellar came back to me in a flash. The lightbulb in the stairwell. All those jars. Those gardens—I made room for another garden so those foster parents could force George, a young child, to eat hot peppers from their garden as a means of discipline; so I heard later.

In graduate school, they don't teach you to be human—you learn this early on if you're lucky, and you continue to learn it, hopefully. Do we ever learn it completely, though? Why didn't I see it? There is silence. There are habits and routines people have. And there are moral and ethical codes we must follow. Facts and facades. Why couldn't I tell something was going on with George and fix it? I wonder who discovered this or if George finally said, *No!*

All this education, I think, and I never stopped once to ask him, *Is everything okay?*

Little Red Love Machine

We learned to French kiss at Skateworld. We wanted to be Men at Work but were—more specifically on Friday and Saturday nights—boys with boners. Michael Jackson was the King of Pop, and we worshipped him. We could reenact the whole fourteen minute *Thriller* video—zombies and all. We proudly wore our white sequined gloves on our right hands until Scott Lumber, a second-year tenth-grader, picked us up one after another by our belt loops and pinned us to the lockers for wearing them.

We owned but hid our Madonna vinyl. Boy George was singing "Karma Chameleon," and I don't think any of us really knew what that song meant, but we loved it. We sang loud, along with Duran Duran, Prince, Morris Day and The Cure. Frankie had been to Hollywood, said to relax, not to do it, but we didn't listen. We had our Jungle Love—our *Owee, Owee, Oh!* Our Sims wheels, jump bars, dance stops and Boeckl—1 1/2 revs, landing backwards on the same foot. On the skating rink, we would cut it up—breakdancing on wheels.

Skateworld advertised family fun, but after the couple's skate during the two-song black out craze, we lined the walls with girls we were "going with" *or* "going out with." Our skates made us half-a-foot taller as we pushed in close—palm against palm—lilacs and the sweet smell of sweat for the first time. We rolled our tongues and opened our mouths to the fire and awkwardness of faces and kisses colliding. Words whispered to us…*let's try something new…put it here—no, here. Yes.* Our shaking hands busily trying to find treasures we couldn't make out in the dark. Our bodies quivering for the occasion. When the lights blasted back on, the wheels were still turning, and our too-bright faces revealed themselves. We looked around for the right words to say, but never at eye level.

Donnie Ansel might then jump a foot out of the rink—both skates airborne—up onto the carpet, retrieve his skate case from a wall of lockers where we hid our belongings and then back-skate his way to the restroom so he could change his shirt. We would follow. This was hip. We would bring half a drawer of clothes with us to swap or lose forever. In the restroom we would drown ourselves in Polo cologne and talk of our new adventures—the curve of breasts in our sweaty hands, tongues in mouths and tongues in our ears. We might even ask a question of someone we really could confide in—"Hey, what am I supposed to do when I have my hand down there?" We would adjust our tight jeans. Guys would spray their big hair with someone's mom's Aqua Net they had swiped. Check the contours of their crotches—while simultaneously sizing each other up. We would return to the rink, new chameleons ready and eager to learn more. During the week, we would dream, polish our skates— wait impatiently to return—dust the furniture and vacuum the floor so we could earn allowance money to go again and again.

"What happened to your purple and pink Izod I bought for you the other day?" my mother asked one day.

"Donnie Ansel's borrowing it."

"Who the hell is Donnie Anslam?"

"Ansel, mom—Donnie Ansel. Not Anslam!" I hollered as I stormed out of my room. "You're always getting my friends' names wrong."

For a while, this worked. What I didn't want was my mom to ask too many questions. I knew my mother rummaged through my things. She was a neat freak. This is a woman who has been known to put decorative pebbles in her potted plants, so people won't see the dirt. Everything was in order. If I left my shoes by the front door, she'd holler for me to put them in my closet. She was always suspicious. And to top it off, she didn't like the fact that girls were starting to call our house to ask if I was going skating. But more than likely, she would take and pick me up from Skateworld the following week, and I'd make sure I got the purple and pink Izod back—that the Copenhagen and the jar of vodka I had swiped from my dad were gone from my skate case. This went on for a good two years—the clothing, tobacco, occasional booze and any other materials we thought might make us look good to the opposite sex.

"Jimmy, where's my Prince tape?" my dad asked in a fever one day. "The one with that Red Corvette song on it." And I knew what would come next, which always came after my father searched frantically for a song he wanted to hear—he would try and sing it himself:

...It was Saturday night
I guess that makes it all right
And you say what have I got to lose?
And honey I say
Little red corvette
Bah ahh wair nair

He held on to the last lyrics while wanking out an imaginary guitar solo in my bedroom. After he came to, he looked at me squarely. "Have you seen it?"

"I gave it to Kelly Hillside."

"Kelly who?"

"Hillside."

"A girl. Right. Okay then." My father scratched his shoulder. "Makes sense. Get it back. I want it back."

"Kelly is a guy."

"What? Get my damn tape back, you hear me!" And he boogied his way out of my room. Down the hall I heard him still singing;

Move over baby
Gimme the keys
I'm gonna try to tame your little red love machine! Ahh haa!

"And another thing"—he stormed back into my room to make his point. "Quit stealing my vodka and putting water in the bottle. You hear me? You think I can't taste that?"

Sexuality wasn't an issue in my house growing up. I never felt uncomfortable talking about it or reading about it in one of my father's *Penthouse* magazines he kept underneath his bed. Apparently my mother gave me the birds and bees talk, although I don't remember it. She does, and has since told me that I didn't have a lot of questions. Perhaps that is because, as an only child, I spent weeks in the summer at my cousin's house glued to the *Playboy* channel while those in charge played cribbage and smoked out of a bong. It was the early eighties, and everyone was trying hard to hold onto peace and love. Every once in a while, an adult would holler out to us in the living room—"You boys okay in there?" We were speechless, eyes fixated on the television, and that seemed to suit everyone just fine.

Once, I asked my cousin how babies were made—this must have come before the talk with my mother. I remember it vividly. We were in his mother's kitchen, likely taking out the trash or scrounging for another turkey leg. My youngest cousin pointed to the linoleum floor littered with paisley and pansies and said, "It's simple. If a woman was to walk in here and you were to pee on the floor at the same time she was in here that would get her pregnant."

For years, I had a phobia about peeing in public or in any building where a woman might be. "What's a matter, Jimmy, you gotta go?" my father would ask.

"No. No," I would scream as I crossed my legs, searching fearfully for females.

It was Skateworld and the mysterious question box in sixth grade mandatory sex education class that furnished me with the truth. We all gawked and bellered when a lot of anonymous questions were asked—*Can I still have a kid with only one nut?* Mr. Palmly read this out loud to the class, like he read every question, but he couldn't even keep a straight face. As we all laughed and rolled around the room, it was Charlie Ferguson who didn't budge from his seat—who sat still as a mannequin, engulfed in fear. In all of his absolutes, Charlie Ferguson had a concern—right down to the core of his identity and wasn't afraid to ask it. The darkness of questions buried inside a box became magically visible to us. Nothing was hidden—the lights were on.

When Mr. Palmly got ahold of himself, and us, he said firmly, "Yes! Yes, you can still father a child." And Charlie Ferguson never stopped smiling. You have to respect a guy like that.

Maybe that was the beginning—when we realized the only man in the room wasn't our teacher, rather it was the kid who had the ball to ask the bigger question. And Skateworld is where we asked and explored and tried to discover for ourselves what love, lust, or rather, infatuation, was. We donned our tight Lee Jeans and Vans—collars stiff and up. We spiked our hair and decorated our clothing with safety pins. This is where weird science began—forever looking up to the women we adored.

Part of this place we can never give up. We went from break-dancing, skates and boards to college and children of our own. Our audience has grown smaller, but some of us still aren't afraid to get down on the linoleum and back-spin. No one is clapping, though. Our wives simply lower their heads and blush while our children join us on the ground, yelling—"Spin me, daddy! Spin me like that!"

Grandpa, "What's it like to kill another man?"

I remember standing over my grandfather's bed in a *Comfort Living* nursing home in Panama City, Florida. When I massage his bony shoulder, he doesn't say anything. His mouth is open, and he is in considerable pain—shaking constantly. My mother is trying to feed him some water from one of those enormous plastic containers all hospitals and nursing homes have. My grandmother, who has Alzheimer's, pushes her wheelchair two feet and reaches for some Mother's Day cards she received in the mail.

The doctors have him on a steady supply of morphine. I doubt he could pick the plastic container up on his own, nor could he keep a Dixie cup steady. This is a man who has never had a problem eating; he's the same guy who would initiate races at the dinner table to see who could finish first. "Cecil, stop it! He's going to choke," I remember my grandmother griping.

"Ah, Ma, if he goes to war, he won't have time to eat."

My grandfather, Cecil Brandenburg, doesn't look the same as he does in the black and white photos next to his bed. There are two. One I had enlarged and cropped, him in his fishing boat on his friend Russ's boat dock at Leisure Lake. In the other, he's shirtless, punched-up barrel-chest and macho, in whitey-tighty shorts and brown loafers, with me, probably ten, learning to drive his Sears riding lawnmower. I look scared and excited, trying to make a turn to avoid the ditch I'm headed for. I can hear him hollering through the picture. "These are your wheels, Junior. Make that turn."

I see the cabin in the background of the photo. Every summer, I lived with my grandparents on Leisure Lake, outside of Trenton, Missouri, in a place we called a cabin—his retirement home, that he spent years building himself with the help of squirrels like me.

Though at the time I was old enough to know better than to use the leftover gallon-and-a-half of tan house paint to customize his beat-up GM pickup, my grandfather, who was spray painting the truck's paneling with high-gloss brown he had left over from the gutters, insisted that I utilize the same brush I'd used on the garage to paint the cab, doors and rust.

"This truck has a lot of life left in her yet."

When men have their hands on cans of spray paint, they go to a different world, a place where everyone's an artist.

"A little bit more here and here. Shine her up like new," he said. For most of the afternoon, we painted and then watched the truck dry.

"Lookee here; pretty as a plate. Can't even see the streaks," he said. "Ma will be tickled. Matches the house and everything."

"You know," my grandmother Betty says, still holding the Mother's Day cards, "you were always our little boy." My eyes swell with tears, and I walk to their tiny bathroom to find some Kleenex.

Three years ago, we moved my grandparents' possessions from their retirement home into my parent's dining room and the spare bedroom. We took their essentials, boxes that were duct-taped and labeled "Must Have" and "Take": his favorite chair, my grandmother's antique blue Royal Copenhagen plates, silver predating the First World War, the television set, a homemade rock grinder and polisher—an assortment of shells and craft accessories, family pictures, photo albums, a double-barreled double-hammer shotgun, two rifles, boxes of puzzles, and some cypress tree coffee tables my grandfather handmade. I remember buying the six-inch-thick slices of cypress from the side of the highway in Mississippi at an early age. Every few years, before I was a teenager, my grandparents would take me down through the Deep South on our way to Florida to collect shells and other necessities to make their crafts, which they sold in shopping malls and craft fairs across the Midwest. And, more importantly, to dine and experience, "Real folk, Junior."

After my grandparents moved to my parents' place in Omaha, Nebraska, they wound up lost in South Dakota one evening, after getting the oil changed in their car that afternoon just two miles from my parent's house. They eventually found their way back, but not until the next day. The police came and tried to reason and ask questions about their whereabouts. After that incident, and some spells of medical trauma, we packed their belongings again and moved them into an assisted-living home. We left my grandfather's rifles and shotguns hidden underneath the basement stairwell, against his will.

And now, a few years later, my own parents are moving to Kansas City, and I inherit the guns. When I look through the gun cases, a worn black Rolf's wallet falls out. I know it's my grandfather's although there is no ID. Inside are seventeen paper dollars and three silver dollars, one for each of his daughters—I'm sure of this—and an Enderlin Diamond Jubilee token celebrating the North Dakota town's 75th anniversary. The token is good for fifty cents at all Enderlin banks until July 31, 1966.

I come to realize that this is his secret stash, the secret stash he has forgotten about or misplaced. Or perhaps it's the one that triggered the dementia, this disease, this loneliness of memory. I find his wedding picture folded and creased five times—a black and white of my grandmother and him on the steps of The Little Brown Church. The pastor is smiling; everyone is smiling, my grandfather chinless with glee and my grandmother standing tall, grinning, her slip exposed. I try to keep the picture unfolded as I gently slip it into one of the wallet's plastic picture sleeves.

What I've been told from other family members in the last few years is this: my grandfather didn't stick around long enough to receive his pension—he quit his night job as a plate-setter at the city newspaper two months before reaching full retirement to go live off the land. That's one version I'm not particularly buying. I didn't ask any more questions about it. It seems the older I get someone's always got a story about someone close to them, and it's always a one-sided version.

Every once in a while he'd bring home a plate from his job at the Des Moines *Register*—a sheet of aluminum with a particularly important story on it for us to keep. I have one in my office—a cartoon titled "In Good Old U.S.A." that illustrates hard work—and that hard work equals the American Dream—as long as you aren't hanging out at the corner drugstore, the sky's the limit on what you can accomplish. This is a belief he instilled in me. He was always working or piddling with something. I rarely saw the man sit. He enjoyed work. Like most men his age, he put in his time, whether he always liked it or not. Why quit with only two months to go? He has some VA disability benefits he collects, a little social security, but not nearly as much as is needed. His plan to live off the land in the home he built on Leisure Lake didn't pan out. My grandmother, for most of her life, was a homemaker—she tended to the daily chores and waited on him, and she seemed to love it. They were, by God, a couple who loved each other deeply.

My grandfather always told me that the government owed him money. What is true or not doesn't matter now. When he does get to talking about the war, about what the government owes him, it's not particularly amusing.

"I can be an old, mean sonofagun. I know that. My union pension pissed down the toilet, and I'm still waiting for money from the government so I can retire in style. After my call to duty, I worked forty-five years as a plate setter for Capital City and nothing to show for it now except a free subscription for my memories. I fought overseas, killed men I was programmed to eliminate. Got my Morse code tooth, the one that took me on secret missions, pulled out—no proof now that I was ever in any godforsaken war.

"I used to get a *tap tap tap* coming by satellite on my back right molar. They came in fifteen-second intervals. Codes were given and instructions followed on the nearest land phone. Can you imagine having a goddamn telegram going off in your mouth for forty years? Well, I can, but now no one believes a word I say."

It's always the same static, the same details that keep me intrigued with an ear bent in his direction. He has always been a good storyteller—no one is denying him that. Now, what, though? Sitting and waiting, I suppose, for his next *tap tap tapping* to come in. This mysteriousness and unknowability is coupled with what this man has meant to me all my life. I've always wanted to believe everything he says to me. People contradict people all the time. And I can understand that. Why did my grandfather lose his pension? Does he really have a radio tooth? How does war affect men? I don't think my grandfather's core is unreachable—he is loving and outgoing—he talks to strangers any chance he gets. He loves to tell his stories. He probably annoys the hell out of some people. This has all rubbed off on me. I love to talk, and my terrible habit of interrupting people comes from him. I call it only-child syndrome. Anticipation of human communication. This overwhelming excitement to run my mouth stems from a paranoid sense of urgency to both fix the world and not leave anything boxed up in case I spontaneously combust.

My grandfather is a man more fully present and alive than most men I look up to and learn from. I look up to him because he listens to me. It's crucial to know you are being listened to as you try to learn and, like I've heard from elders so many times before, broaden your horizons. I never knew I owned a horizon, but I guess I do as much as the next guy. And on the days when I think too much, staring out into the vast openness of these Great Plains of ours, I ponder all of this—do we really remember what we tell our children? How much do we internalize and think we've told them? How much do we forget to tell those closest to us? These are questions worth asking yourself. My grandfather gave me rein to explore more than anyone else. He tried to understand my world. He didn't just tell me what to do and act as some *Father Knows Best* character.

I can see him shirtless in his worn jeans and belt cinched tight as I watch him climb an old oak tree in his front yard. I toss him a worn-handled hacksaw with rusted teeth, ask him why pruning is necessary. I watch him twist his limbs among the tree's, lose himself and land flat on his back. I hover over him screaming, *Grandpa! Grandpa! You dead?* Later that night, in the garage, I snoop through *Playboys* my father gave him, hear the toil and mince of ax on grinder, saws sharpening, and that goddamn tree. *I'll fix that son-of-a-bitch.*

Years later, there was this recession from life—from me. His dwindling. The disease taking more of him away, although I was unaware of it. I had started a family of my own, too, and wasn't around much. As the dementia, or as other family members say, "Can't remember shit," set in, we were all planning an extended-family trip to the lake. It happened to fall on one of the first weekends when we found out my wife was pregnant with our first child. I threw my pond-hopper bass boat, "The Other Woman," into the bed of our Chevy S10 and headed down to Missouri.

The blacktop hilly-backroads wind in all directions, and I was eager to get down to Leisure Lake to tell my grandparents the good news first. My wife was turning a little green in the seat next to me. I hadn't fully grasped that a human was growing inside her body, and these roads I was now navigating weren't the best accommodations for her. "Slow down. I'm not giving birth today." I knew when we arrived my grandfather and I would fish, and here I could tell him the good news. For some reason, I was compelled to tell my grandmother the news before him, though. We approached the few acres, about a mile from the lake, where the house was. In my mind, I still see a little slab of concrete and a pop-up trailer, which eventually turned into a typical 1200 foot ranch house with a patio and wood deck. The house has a detached workshop and garage where I spent most of my time.

I can picture the scene vividly as we stood inside the cabin and my grandmother tried to busy herself. Something was odd. The curtains were drawn. The cabin, with its wood-paneled walls and floral couch/fold-out bed, seemed dreary. But maybe I was over-analyzing. The bookcase/liquor cabinet was still in its normal place. Great leather-bound novels repackaged by some vanity press lined the shelves. The miniature porcelain man holding a bottle of moonshine on top of the fireplace was in the same spot—if you turned the key a few times, it would sing "How dry I am, How dry I am," over and over. There were puzzle pieces spread across a green fold-up table. On another table were seashells—all shapes and sizes—that my grandmother would use to make shadow boxes. The old, large veneer vintage television, stacked with VCR and rabbit-ears antennas, was sinking into the shag carpet.

When we told her, my grandmother paused and smiled. It was awkward, though. As if she either didn't quite understand what I was telling her or she was having flighty thoughts. Within ten seconds or so, she said, "That's wonderful news." But that initial pause startled me. I had just hurried us down to their place—a five hour drive—to tell them the news, and that pause was alarming. Something didn't seem right. I would find out later that weekend that my grandmother was forgetting to make supper. Forgetting to eat. My grandfather, who could barely open a can of beans for himself, didn't know what to do. He could build a house, fillet a fish, but I can't remember ever seeing him cook anything. Now that I think of it, I'm not sure he even used the Weber grill that sat rusting in the garage.

That weekend, other family came down to visit, too. After I had found out about my grandmother's forgetfulness, my grandfather and I went fishing. There was nothing I could do. Besides, we always went fishing. When we were on my little two-seater boat, I looked at him and said, "I know what you're doing Grandpa—you're not fooling me." It was a cocky thing to say, and I wasn't exactly sure what I was accusing him of. But I thought I'd bait him, see how he'd react.

I had assumed he was making some of the story up about my grandmother. He always made stories up. And it was still my job to believe all of them. Was my grandmother really forgetting to cook? Was it too much for him to handle? I had assumed he was out of money because I didn't want to believe what was happening. No one really knew what was going on. But I had seen my grandmother pause in the living room—that was enough to know something wasn't right. I was trying to process what I had seen, what I had heard from various family members, and make my own assumptions about my grandparents' situation. I just couldn't believe people could forget to cook. Something about that story sounded fishy. My grandfather turned to me in the boat, his straw fedora hat cocked to the side. He looked through a pair of busted prescription glasses he had tried to fix and tape up himself, and grinned.

That grin is an image I won't ever forget. It haunts me. My grandfather enjoyed fooling with me. He was a jokester. But this isn't something he could joke about. Which makes me think I was sitting that day in a boat with a man who was deathly afraid to tell me the truth. Everything he had worked for had come to fruition and now as both he and my grandmother were supposed to be enjoying their retirement some basic life skills were getting in their way. I question now if it was a grin, a smirk—a sort of smile, an expression that was meant to say more than words ever could? Maybe that mien was meant to say, *I made it this far Junior. Now look what's happened.*

We sat that day in the middle of the lake for a little while and didn't say much. I wasn't about to row back inland. Part of me wanted to stay put and keep casting. Hell, we could've sat there forever. Two men in the nosebleed section on some small lake outside Trenton, Missouri. Who would miss us? We had fish surrounding us and plenty of lures to keep casting. We were two men in a slowly sinking boat, whether we wanted to believe it or not.

I never told anyone about this. It made me mad. As I got older my grandfather and I butted heads. I didn't always follow his lead. I was all grown up now, with a wife and a child on the way. There were so many dimensions of my life, of our lives, which started on that very lake with bait and a hook. That was as close as we got to communicating some of the tough truths of aging—of dementia. Two men sitting in a boat staring at each other. If I put myself in his shoes, and everything is true, how scared he must have felt to admit the house that he'd built, the dream he had for the both of them, was so quickly slipping away. He knew that day his time there was limited. He was an artist who saw his dreams to completion. I believe now his expression was that of confusion. The truth disguised as fear. I've never been back to fish there since. It was our place. It would seem wrong to fish there without him.

Two of the items my grandfather was proud to give me were a survival knife and sword he had brought back from WWII. The knife I'd seen him carry and use throughout my childhood. It fit in a leather case he strapped to his belt—the name, Brandenburg, burned into the leather hide. The knife blade is six inches long and sharp on one side—the other side is jaded.

The sword is Japanese, a "souvenir" from the war. He'd told me many times that the soldiers could bring back one souvenir from their enemy. Even at an early age, I thought that sounded wrong. The sword hung high up in his garage and makeshift craft room. I remember my cousins and me stacking boxes on top of chairs trying to reach the sword on many occasions—we never could. And one occasion, I remember he took it out of the case and twirled it around and made funny Japanese noises—or noises that sounded foreign to us. We felt the tip of the sword, and it was deadly sharp. He put the souvenir in the case and hung it back up on the wall. I hadn't thought about it until a few years ago when he told my parents to give it to me. The sword now hangs in our garage, high above the worktable in the rafters. One day, my daughters will see it and ask about it, and I will tell its story.

My grandfather didn't mind talking about the war. He was an infantryman in the Army. He was on the front line. Only once, when I was feeling particularly cocky, did I ask him the million dollar question—"Grandpa, what's it like to kill another man?" That evening, he leaned in, looked me firmly in the face and said, "We didn't have a choice. We did what we were told to do." He stared at me for about fifteen seconds and then broke down into tears and walked into the guest room of my parents' house— his new bedroom. I felt ashamed of myself for asking, but I honestly wanted to know—that was something I'd never heard him talk about. In that minute, and for the next few hours, I felt a pain I'd never experienced. A sorrow for the guy I realized I would never fully understand. "We didn't have a choice. We did what we were told to do."

One afternoon, as my grandfather sat dozing in and out of consciousness on my parents' patio, I asked him about the sword. No one was talking, so I thought we could reminisce—talk about fishing, the lake, the sword that now hung in my garage. He perked up and jumped right in. "Well, Junior, it was like this." My grandfather raised himself up in his chair and jabbed his right hand towards me—then he jerked the hand straight up in one swift motion. "And that was that," he said.

My father looked up from the book he was reading and over the tops of his glasses and shook his head at me. "You happy, now?"

My grandfather leaned back down in his chair.

"Not the knife, Grandpa, the sword," I said.

"Oh, that. It was a souvenir from the enemy."

My parents and I take my grandmother for a walk in the nursing home. I've been sizing the place up since we got out of the car. It's nothing compared to the assisted-living facility they were at in Omaha, or my aunt-and-uncle's place in Panama City Beach. It's a screwed-up system that allows people who worked so hard to end up in nursing homes that most people can't stomach for more than an hour or so.

My grandmother can get around well in her wheelchair and seems to enjoy pushing herself around the facility. We pass an elderly woman holding a plastic baby.

"Look," my grandmother says shrewdly, "a baby holding a baby."

The comment doesn't faze the woman as she continues to stare at the plastic doll and comb its hair. We make our way out into a courtyard where a family sits and visits under a tin carport and some teenage kid smokes. The kid looks at the tattoo on my leg and says, "Hey, man. What's up?" He tries to pull himself together. Maybe I remind him of one of his hipster friends. I feel anything but hip right now as I struggle to make conversation. My grandmother comments on the beautiful flowers in the courtyard— they are fake plastic bouquets. My grandmother asks about her great granddaughter, and my mother tells her that I'm a professor now at a college.

"He was always our little boy," she says again. "Always knew he'd be successful."

"Look at this, Grandma." I pull out a business card the college has made for me. "It says *doctor*. Can you believe that?"

She giggles and says she's going to show Cecil when he wakes up. "He'll be so proud."

Taped to the entrance of the "Market Store," there are pictures of a lot of the residents dressed up in Mardi Gras hats and colorful beads. My grandmother is holding onto a hallway railing with the others. She is smiling, and that is nice to see. She points out a fake fish in a fake aquarium in the store window and says, "Oooohh." She still has her sense of humor.

I'd like to tell you we stayed all day at the nursing home and had a grand time. The truth of the matter is that we weren't there for more than an hour or two. My grandfather remained in the darkness of his disease and medication. A few years ago, he was the stronger of the two. Now, she was the one holding it somewhat together. We left and returned later to pick up my grandmother so she could attend my cousin's dance recital. That night, our last in Florida, my grandfather was rushed to the emergency room because he was so dehydrated. Then, stabilized, he went back to the nursing home.

When I left him in his room that day, I wondered if it would be the last time I'd ever see him, his mouth hanging open, eyelashes gone, his moaning in pain. The man in that bed is not the man I picture when I think about visiting my grandparents on those trips to Leisure Lake. I think of the man who built his own retirement home with his bare hands. I think about the thousands of fish we caught, cleaned and ate.

Oftentimes, I picture myself on my grandfather's riding lawnmower—that's how I learned to drive. Other times, I'm walking on the dirt road—the mile down to the lake with my fishing pole, metal stringer and plastic tackle-box in my hand. All these sepia snapshots come to me. Little moments I hold on to. A crazy snapping turtle on my fishing line. A water moccasin swimming towards me on the bank I am standing on. I think about us at dusk, my grandpa Cecil, his soothsayer fishing buddy Russ, and me on all fours hunting night crawlers. They hold flashlights and PBR's as I wait with my tweezer-fingers to attack. "Don't let go, Junior," one says. "That's a keeper, all right." I follow the light beams back and forth, back and forth, attack, squeeze and pull until the night crawler gives or splits in two.

Then I think of the present. Grandpa, it's twenty-five years later, and I'm half a world away. You, skinny as hospital tissue, lying in a nursing home bed. Me, on my knees, crawling in garden rows, searching for crawlers—engulfed in dirt, bull snake and mosquitoes. I will always remember the last time we fished, you looking at me through those taped up glasses. When we did make it to shore, I had to ask for help to lift you from the boat onto the dock, bluegills and bass gone to grass carp the size of Harleys.

These memories will never end. I will carry them with me like I do everything that matters. I still have the stories. And soon I will take the girls fishing. I will tell them about the fish hook in my mother's head, how I saved you from jumping overboard, how we hammered fish for years.

Sleep, Grandpa, sleep. You are the ghost on third, and I'm sending you home.

Man vs. Food

I'm warming up on the elliptical machine at the fitness center, feeling adequate next to the large man moving ever so slowly and uneasily on the stationary bike next to me. And I am in control of the remote for once, watching *Man vs. Food*.

"Is this show really necessary?" the large man barks. "Give me that remote."

I turn up the volume, reassure him that it is necessary, that if the host can consume the Italian Challenge—seven pounds of chicken parmesan, Italian sausage, lasagna, spaghetti and meatballs, manicotti, a whole loaf of garlic bread, fresh salad, cannelloni, a cup of Italian wedding soup, and an apple crisp dessert in under ninety minutes, he wins a t-shirt. "Only been done two times," I add, "ever." Increasing my resistance, I watch my heart rate peak.

On the track now, I'm running my three miles, like I do most nights. Routine, mundane, and all nine-minute mile splits. I can't seem to go faster. Round, pale-white men from a group home arrive in swim trunks pulled too high on their bellies and cannonball into the pool like kids fresh off the bus on summer break. Their supervisor waves to the lifeguard on duty who absently spins his whistle around his finger. Some of the men grab bright rubber basketballs and shoot hoops. Some beam with laughter and mouths full of water, becoming underwater people.

One twenty-something man always slips into the shallow end and squats, his chest and thighs pressed tightly together. Left arm acting as a ladle, he scoops a handful of water, raises it over his head and, fingers dangling, pours a slow spigot of chlorine down into his cupped right hand. Tonight, he cocks his head to the left, where the swim team practices the backstroke, balancing plastic pop bottles on their foreheads. Exercises in grace that look so easy from a distance. *See*, he seems to say. *Do you see that? How beautiful we are.*

I stop to catch my breath. I'm 46 years old. No longer as graceful as I picture myself. My body glistens with sweat. There's some grey in my hair. My daughters are on the verge of braces and breaking rules. Everything, I guess, right on time.

Reading Harry Potter and the Chamber of Secrets

"There are worse crimes than burning books.
One of them is not reading them."
— Joseph Brodsky

I was excited when my 10 ½ year old daughter asked me if we could read the book out loud to each other, alternating pages. "A chapter a night," she proclaimed. My older daughter, who is 14 ½ and drives with a restricted license, has outgrown bedtime stories, but I still remember tearing through *Year 1* with her and am happy to pick up the series again.

On the pages, we empathize with Harry. "*Happy birthday to me… happy birthday to me…*" *No cards, no presents, and he would be spending the evening pretending not to exist.* And we feel sorry and not so bad when we laugh at Dudley who *…was so large his bottom drooped over either side of the kitchen chair…"Pass the frying pan."* And don't forget Moaning Myrtle—the ghost who lives in her out-of-order bathroom. All these years, the strange noises coming from bathrooms—the moaning always suspect, but I've never seen a Myrtle.

When I met Megan McDonald, author of the Judy Moody series, at the South Dakota Festival of Books, I introduced myself and told her I couldn't leave until I had her signature and a selfie with her. "Daughter's orders. She knew the both of us would be here." She laughed and told me that she'd been at a grade school in California recently and asked all the students to bring a book from home the next day. She would be visiting with them again and was curious to see what they were reading. A large majority of the students showed up the next day and were hesitant to share—a lot of them had brought magazines from home with the covers ripped off. She showed me a statistic on her phone that shocked me. "Children from middle-income homes have on average 13 books per child. There is only 1 book for every 300 children in low-income neighborhoods."[13]

It's a delight, listening to my daughter articulate some brilliant sentences, reading confidently, so excited to enter this made-up world and the magic of black words on white paper, both of us laughing together at the right times.

When we are done with our 15 pages, I tell Paige, "Thanks for reading with me."

"Can we read tomorrow night?" she asks.

"You bet. We are going to read all of them."

"Yeah!"

At the Eight-Hour Work Meeting with Bathroom Breaks and a Light Lunch Provided

You watch a glass of water in front of you perspire. A tapping foot under the table—another nervous twitch. The blonde in the tight skirt next to you scribbles *Born To Be Wild* on a yellow legal pad and yawns.

"Well, we all know what the real elephant in the room is," trumpets the man in charge. "Let's not be off a hitch here." He waves his right arm flush with the vast horizon outside the huge picture window, which seems so distant now. "Let's calibrate." His good 'ol boy vernacular continues, all the while grinning like a mule eatin' briars. It's clear to you that the pachyderm in the room is standing on his last leg—reaching. "I'm astonished at the elements of power this position entails."

"They're just window dressing," a VP says, sitting up straighter, reassured and red-faced in the posh chair. The designer leather elbow pads of his sports jacket act as suction cups as he tries to raise his arms to emphasize his point.

Under her breath, the blonde says, "At least they know how to dress!" She checks her text messages and drops her vibrating iPhone into her lap.

There's a charge in the room. Or was that an ass suffocating a seat? The fake plastic plant in the corner of the room looks dead.

You look out the window. You remember stopping once in Erwin, Tennessee, where legend has it they hung the circus elephant 'Big Mary' with a crane large enough to lift locomotive boilers. She had stomped her trainer. Erwin, now known as the town that hung the elephant. You Google Big Mary because you are thinking of showing the picture of the elephant to the woman next to you. The roadsideamerica.com article reads: "Over 5,000 spectators showed up to watch the elephant hanging. Big Mary was positioned beneath the crane and then yanked aloft by a chain around her neck—which promptly broke and sent her plummeting to the concrete, knocking her unconscious. A daring spectator, not wanting to disappoint the crowd, dashed forward and reattached the chain. Big Mary was hoisted again, and this time, justice was done." You remember the Hanging Elephant Antique Gallery once sold Big Mary t-shirts. You're pretty sure, although the town has established a nearby elephant sanctuary, you will never go back there.

"We need a little steak with all this sizzle!" A razor-burned neck says, snapping and cracking as if to re-emphasize a toughness rooted deep within the spine. Without fuss, a small astute man stands.

"We've sent out the samples and have to wait until we get the results of the feelers."

"The feelers," someone mumbles. A few people nod their heads.

You reach for your full glass of water, tiny ice crystals slowly dissecting themselves from the last large, transparent cube that has risen to the top and slowly grown thin, all of the particles falling away gracefully, free and forever into a clear unknown.

Degrees of Love–Pieces at Twenty Years

It was a Sunday afternoon, overcast. We sat in that Catholic retreat center doodling on our clipboards, adding our own engravings next to the others who had come before us—next to *Jake Loves Michelle FOREVER!* and *THIS PLACE SUCKS, I'd rather be in HELL!*

That Sunday, we sat and listened to a priest question his faith and life choices. How he still remembers his high school sweet-heart—how he is experienced some himself, and how he has sinned and repented. How he wonders what she might be doing now.

Two-hundred dollars is what we paid to swap quiz-bowl-questions and talk about our feelings with other soon-to-be newlyweds. This is where you were told to let it all out. On the back of the door in the men's room, someone stuck a sign up that read, *There's no turning back now, Jack!*

It was at this weekend-retreat that we watched a wide-eyed natural planner talk to us about making babies, he and his wife's swing set, cycles and the odd days of the month. And I wanted to say then, *I do believe we are all created equal—just some of us screwed together a little looser or tighter than others. I do believe it's a good idea to own a dog before you ever think of raising a child of your own. I think everyone at least once, should ride shotgun in a loaded grain truck with spotty brakes. I believe it might slow people down a bit. I do believe, but have my fair share of questions. I do believe that priest should get on a bus and find his high school sweetheart. For better or worse, I do.*

* * *

How did you meet your wife? The short answer: in college.

I had been trailing her for a couple of years—privately, like most stalkers do. When the situation arose, I picked up a telephone and asked her if I could walk her to class. We had shared a few literature classes together, so I wasn't a complete stranger to her. She wore blue sweat-pants and a light-grey sweatshirt that she turned inside out—running shoes that she utilized. My friend, a former classmate of hers, said, "You're just the rebound guy. You are polar opposites. She's an athlete. You're not."

I walked her to class the next day. It sounds more romantic than it was. She didn't live all that far from the building she needed to get to. I was nervous but also euphoric that she hadn't hung up the phone on me the night before. We later went on official dates. I wish I would have told my friend that we all rebound. I mean, tell me a first love that didn't break your heart. I never said anything. I made him an usher in our wedding instead.

* * *

Some words my wife hates in no particular order: Bangs. Crotch. Slacks. Blouse. Toppings. Crafty. Moist. Outfit. Discuss. FYI. Blasé. Hunky-Dory. Pamphlets. An expression she doesn't care for: "I'm fixin' to do something." "Attend," she says, "is a wimpy word."

An award-winning participant in high school speech contests, she doesn't like to be read to. As a writer who is oftentimes anxious to share my latest creation aloud, this can be frustrating.

"Would you mind reading this new poem?"

How long is it?

"I just want your feedback."

Every time I tell you what I think you get all pissed off.

"You're exaggerating."

Uh-huh. You really want me to tell you what I think?

"Please. Usually when you don't like it, it gets published."

Isn't that nice. Stir the sauce, it's starting to burn.

"What?"

In front of you—the sauce. And don't let the noodles boil too long.

"What about this line…Free those breasts and their veiny road maps…"

Stop. I hate when you read it to me out loud. Just give me the damn thing.

"Not if you're going to get all pissy about it."

Fine.

"Great. The noodles are all soggy."

I told you.

Sometimes after a grueling day of work she says, "There were all kinds of bad things running through my head today, but I kept them to myself. It could have gotten ugly."

The other day I was talking about marketing a new manuscript of mine, and she said, "Your books will sell when you're dead. That's the way that works."

These absolutes are why I love her.

* * *

One of those first Friday nights, staring at my inadequate paycheck, I couldn't stop shaking. The bills were due, and I wasn't holding enough in my hands. This was twenty years ago, 11th and E. Street, where we moved from college to careers—small town to city. I can still see the dim lights of that shoebox of an apartment. One old Murphy bed closet that held everything we owned, where we hid our useless college degrees and hung her brand-new wedding dress. Our used college textbooks and dual copies of *Beloved* and *Crime and Punishment*, a couple of great novels on our bookcase. Our wool socks snagging on the splintered wooden floor. The un-insulated plaster walls that ached with the wind—water pipes that popped and gurgled in the cold. Such character I thought, with its sconce wall lights and barefoot-claw tub. Sirens and another aimless wanderer outside on the street, sounds that never turned off.

Did we really hate the woman upstairs who partied late nights after her bar shift? I questioned my own bohemian lifestyle, the one I had read so much about—where pain and suffering were part of the process. Me, a wannabe-writer who hadn't done much yet, pleading with the day-shift manager for $7.50 an hour. I'd made more money in high school, telemarketing Omaha Steaks, than I did with a college degree.

We sat at our first computer in a porch room that wasn't heated, typing resumes, trying to type poetry, our story, and their story—our graduate school applications. Always that throb of my heart in my eyelids that I just wanted to turn off, voices rattling in my head, waking me most nights in a hot sweat. The hellish nightmare that was my life, working in a warehouse, maintaining an Optical Character Reader, sorting endless flats, smothered in meter machines.

Some nights, I still see myself sitting on that floral yellow-and-green, hand-me-down couch with my head in my hands. I see you standing there, radiant, confident that we would get by. Maybe that was the night I started to believe that even with all my dreams and disillusionment, it would work. You and I. The faith you had in me picked me up like it's done so many times.

* * *

It bothers me when I see my wife get off from a twelve-hour shift, come home and lie lifeless on the couch. Losing herself in the television. Sometimes curling up in a ball. When I ask her how work was, she says, "We got our asses handed to us. People died. Same old shit."

What I'm learning is, there is nothing I can say or do. I will never know what it's like to watch a twenty-two-week-old baby hang on for three more months, then die. Will never know what it's like to scrape dead flesh from burnt living bodies. Will never know what it's like to rise at five a.m. and stay on my feet until seven p.m. without much break, without lunch, and, god willing, without error. Will never know what it feels like to turn code, stabilize, and then realize *I've forgotten one easy last step*. Will never know the satisfaction of flying to Kentucky or Idaho, from Nebraska—in a twin prop—to bring a baby back to life. Will never know what it's like, except this: "We got our asses handed to us. People died."

* * *

A woman sitting across from us in the emergency room is losing it into a small gray tub while talking on her cell phone. I am not losing it yet, nor is my daughter, Willow, who is here to lose the pea stuck deeply up into her nasal cavity. Nor is my wife, who would be here on duty if this weren't her night off.

> *Inflate a balloon and tie it off. Let a little air out before tying it completely. This way it will be easier to pop the balloon without breaking it. The balloon should not be longer than the needle.*

My daughter sneezes, but no pea. She continues to throw playing cards on the cold ceramic tile. A woman in white scrubs comes to take us in.

> *Dip the entire needle or sharp skewer in some sort of cooking oil.*

The doctor laughs,

> *In a gentle manner—insert the needle into the nipple end of the balloon.*

asks my wife, "Isn't this your night off?" He goes in with an inflatable needle, a device that looks like a needle, but once inserted and is past the intruder, the tip expands.

Continue pushing, twisting and turning the needle or skewer until you puncture the opposite side of the balloon (near the tied end). Continue to pull the needle out near the tied end—the balloon will slowly lose air.

The doctor's hands move precisely and slowly; the pea, still green and solid, is freed.

Once the needle is free, jab the balloon.
The balloon will pop.

* * *

"How do you like my M's?" my wife asks. "They are supposed to be birds. How about my purple horse?" It's bedtime for Willow, November 1. We are grilling and drinking day-old Vampire wine. Chalk on the bricks. A game of tic-tac-toe—no winner, no loser. Sunshine, XXOOXO, and a bizarre looking fish. The sidewalk art glows with glee. My daughter's sand-box toys are strewn across the yard. It's nine o' clock and, for two more hours, if Willow doesn't wake, this time is ours. The cool buzz of the baby monitor, the cheesy brats bursting on the grill, the gurgle and kiss.

* * *

It's my wife's birthday, and she's pregnant. She's crying. She's only thirty-four. She's a knock-out. "It's your birthday," I say. "You can't cry on your birthday."

"It's my birthday, and I'll cry if I want to."

I start in on my own rendition of Lesley Gore's teen queen hit.

It's my party, and I'll cry if I want to,
cry if I want to, cry if I want to.

She doesn't find me amusing. She says I just don't understand. My wife wants a party, she doesn't want a party. She doesn't want the mess I've promised to clean up. She wants peach pie. Maybe chocolate.

"Where's the damn chocolate in this house? If I die and you marry another woman, make sure she's a good mother. You hear me?"

* * *

It is spring again, young mothers. Valentines have been sent.
The front doors are ajar—little faces press against storm door
glass. Put away the disinfectant wipes, and come out, come out. Fill
porches with laughter. Bring your mending hearts and concerns.
Free those breasts for these little creatures to discover. And let this
be a thank you from all of us who dart off to work—reluctant to
look in our rearview mirrors—who oftentimes forget to tell you
how much it all really means.

* * *

Paige, you are only four-weeks-old, and your sister demands she
help out. I hope you know how proud she is wiping dry skin she calls
crumbs from your face, proclaiming to paint another red, white and
black design you can stare at. Before that, though, your mother puts
the finishing touches on the barn she has built in the living room to
house the ponies—blackie Morgan, brown Spirit and white Joe. I
reinforce the support beams, but can't for the life of me figure out
how to secure the ladder to the loft. Some people might think it odd,
a barn in the living room—let them think whatever they like. The
creatures awake early here. Willow galloping with colts, fillies and
foal across wood floors. Your eyes open ever so slowly to peek at this
parade of wild animals.

In between rides and morning breakfast, Willow checks, then
checks again, to see if you are awake. When she finds your eyes
open, she cannot contain herself: "Look, Daddy, Paige is smiling!"

Then back to the Mustangs she trots, taming first one, then
another, waiting as only a child can wait for the time when they can
do the tending, tugging and pulling together.

* * *

My wife re-reads grocery lists, our daughters' progress reports,
medical test results, but rarely wants to read a poem more than once.
This morning she points to a poem in the newspaper, laughs and
says, "This is good." Twice. It's the kind of work people really read
and carry into their comfortable silences. And I wonder, what's a guy
have to do to get a re-read?

This poem about the country girl who is obviously falling for
the strong, unkempt, determined college-boy bumpkin with his arms

full of notebooks and flies buzzing about his head. Proof that I wasted a lot of years presuming what a woman wants. But perhaps a bit of that unkempt boy carrying all the great ideas of the world and starry-eyed song lyrics resembles just a bit of me, that strange, long-haired city-boy she married almost twenty years ago.

I haven't learned much more since then, my notebooks still scribbled with stained pages. I know that the trash is mine to take out, that the heavy lifting and schlepping of large objects is my job. I'm still learning to listen with my two good ears, not the one in between. Maybe city boys never fully understand the significance of flies, that a JD 3020 is a tractor not a new brand of fortified wine, can't distinguish a Hereford from an Angus, but we know when to take our shirts off and how to take our time.

* * *

It's tourney time, and my daughter, Willow, has just scored her second run this season—the innings Mercy Rule follows. Team Thunder hits the field as I strap the catcher's gear onto one of the unlucky players. She's already drenched. It's ninety degrees, muggy as all get-out—a storm brewing. My wife is in the stands, making faces at me, which is always a good sign, and our other daughter, Paige, is chasing ground squirrels with the other kids too young to play ball.

I'm helping coach and keep score with two other fathers as the girls open up their first can of whoop-ass against the opposing team.

"We fetchin' or catchin' here, girls?" the eight-year-old third baseman hollers. And 1,2,3 we are back to the top of our line-up, and the chatter begins.

Can you turn around like Michael Jackson?
Break down like Britney Spears?
Shake it off like Salt-N-Pepa?
No. You Can't!

With cheeks full of sunflower seeds, these girls are starting to gel. How beautiful it is to see them come together as a team, discovering the beauty of the game before it's ruined by adults.

* * *

Tonight after a trip for ice cream, I water the red maple, the first tree we've ever planted. The girls run and chase fireflies. When they catch one, they can't help but hold it hostage and pull its wings. "I just can't stand to see it suffer," Willow says. She grabs the hose and begins drowning the thing. Soon enough they are off for a new adventure. As

I watch my new As-Seen-on-TV Pocket Hose ravel itself into a ball, I catch a glimpse of what's left of the firefly—its cold light smeared on cement, and I hear on this particularly quiet night, the flurry of small wings ascending.

* * *

The other day, my wife said, "We are getting along better than we ever have." And we are. So we got that going for us. It's something that might take some couples a whole lifetime to find.

A friend asked me one time if I knew how to spell love. I looked at her like you might imagine. "Go on," she said, "spell it." So I did.

"L O V E," I said.

"No, that's wrong," she said. "W O R K."

* * *

One of my favorite memories is driving a familiar highway—I could feel Linda looking at me. She turned the radio down and asked, "What are you thinking?" She really wanted to know. I knew I'd ask her to marry me then for sure.

* * *

I can't remember the words you spoke that night over twenty years ago as I sat in our cramped apartment—when you gave me your hand and then turned us to the door, took that antique doorknob and opened it. We walked downtown into the nightlife and danced our blues and my shame away. How little we seemed to have back then. How much love we've surrounded ourselves with now. How we continue to push through the crowd.

Acknowledgments:

My gratitude to the editors of the following publications where the essays (or their beginnings) first appeared:

The Evolutionary Review, Art, Science and Culture: "My Life as Willy the Wildcat" originally published as "What Would Willy Do?"

Lips: (Part of) "Man Vs. Food" appeared as "Right on Time"

MIPOESIAS INVITATIONAL: "Real Mayonnaise" published as "Their Drive to the Funeral"

New Delta Review: "Buckets, Indians and Habaneros"

New York Quarterly Books: (Parts of) "Never Talk to Strangers" originally appeared as poems or stanzas in Reese's books *Dancing Room Only, Really Happy!* and *ghost on 3rd*

The New Territory: "The Mother-in-Law Archives"

Nidus: "MIDWEST Heartland/MID Heart WEST Land" originally published as "Cat Scratch Fever"

Patterson Literary Review: "Little Red Love Machine" originally published as "Hard"; "At the Eight-Hour Work Meeting with Bathroom Breaks and a Light Lunch Provided"; "Grandpa, What's It Like to Kill Another Man"; (Parts of) "Degrees of Love" is Winner of the 2018 Allen Ginsberg Poetry Award

Really Happy (New York Quarterly Books) "Ready, Action!," "SD Bumper Stickers," appeared as poems in the book

South Dakota Review: "Sasquawk and Copenhagen," "How to Become a Regular," "Old Man George and the Chrysler Sebring (A Midwest Journal)" originally appeared as "Old Man George Rides Again"

St. John the Baptist Church—100 Year History: An excerpt of "Bone Chalk" first appeared as "The Great Escape"

These Trespasses (The Backwaters Press) "Willing and Ready," (Parts of) "All the Warning Signs Were Posted," (Parts of) "Never Talk to Strangers" originally appeared as poems

Recently I had the chance to listen to author Alice Sebold talk about her work of nonfiction. At one point she said, "My work squares with but does not duplicate your sense of what happened." I agree. I remember what I remember, and I hope in the telling of my stories that my recollections square with the memories of the people who were involved. Although this is a work of nonfiction, the names of those mentioned have often been changed. Sometimes the characters are amalgamations of various people. Most importantly, the things that moved me to spend years researching and writing are about discovery, not display.

Thank you to Kent Meyers, Mike Reese and Neil Harrison for their time, patience, steadfast and caring criticism. Kimberly Verhines, Sara Henning and Stephen F. Austin State University Press who opened their door to me, welcomed me in and let me keep my boots on. Thank you for believing in my work. James Engelhardt, for your confidence in my work and the visceral. Ted Kooser, who said to me after a poetry reading—"Jim that poem is an entire Willa Cather book." Thank you, Ted, for always pushing me to write nonfiction and for being a critical reader and friend. Daryl Farmer for always encouraging the early nonfiction work and for lifelong friendship—*Where(ever) We Land*. Maria Mazziotti Gillan—for your *Inimitable Heart* and giving a young poet a chance to travel east and perform when no other editor would. Ray Hammond, *New York Quarterly* and *New York Quarterly Books* for the years of faith in my work and for believing in me. The Lammers and Reese family for their love, patience and letting me tell my stories. Joe Weil, George Bilgere, Jim Daniels, Kevin Clark, David Lee, Don Welch, Bill Kloefkorn, Chuck Bowden, Vivian Shipley, Dave Pichaske, Jonis Agee, Marielle Frigge, Stephanie Schultz, Patrick Hicks, Fran Streff, Christine Stewart, Jon Lauck, Marilyn Johnson, Jamie Sullivan, Dana DeWitt, Rich Lofthus, Cynthia Binder, Dante DiStefano, Kevin Carey, Paul Smith, ML Liebler and Detroit Rock City; Matt Mason—who is doing more for writers in Nebraska than anyone I know; Sarah McKinstry-Brown, Dan Jenkins, Bret Gottschall (www.gotty.com), Lori Walsh and South Dakota Public Radio; Bernie and Katie Hunhoff and *South Dakota Magazine*; Pete Dexter who helped encourage me early on and told me what to work on; Jennifer Widman, Sherry DeBoer and the South Dakota Humanities Council; Grace Cavalieri and *The Poet and the Poem* at the Library of Congress; David Cremean, John Price, Susan Maher; Lauren Tuzzolino and Beth Bienvenu at the National Endowment for the Arts. Thanks to Shanna Ibarolle and Sarah Nizzi for letting me tell a bit of your stories. Thanks to Marc Long and Mount Marty College for a sabbatical which allowed me time to write and finish this book. Jerold Ryken, Danny Flahie, Josh Klimek, Ross Den Herder, Dave "His poetry doesn't even rhyme!" Dannenbring for friendship and listening to me talk shop. Srgt. Javier Murgia for the hundred hours of ride-alongs and encouraging my true-crime writing. To my past and present students at Mount Marty College and the prisons where I teach—thanks for pushing me to practice what I preach. And of course for Linda, Willow and Paige for letting me recite my stories out loud some nights at the dinner table. Abrazos.

Endnotes

Never Talk to Strangers—
12 Years in Prisons and What Criminals Teach Me

1 https://www.wowt.com/home/headlines/Killer-faces-resentencing-in-1990-murder-368620461.html

2 https://uiowa.edu/higheredandsuccessfulreentry/sites/uiowa.edu.higheredandsuccessfulreentry/files/esperian.pdf

3 https://www.bop.gov/about/statistics/statistics_inmate_offenses.jsp

4 http://jimreese.org/wp-content/uploads/2011/02/ghost_on_3rd_review_American_Poetry_Journal.pdf

5 https://www.forbes.com/2009/07/13/best-prisons-cushiest-madoff-personal-finance-lockups_slide.html#30b2b2f3fb6f

6 https://obamawhitehouse.archives.gov/the-press-office/2016/06/10/fact-sheet-white-house-launches-fair-chance-higher-education-pledge

7 https://www.omaha.com/columnists/grace/grace-she-listened-as-baby-sitter-was-murdered-and-she/article_6ed32a35-44a6-5f0b-8647-ce68f280e55f.html

8 https://www.washingtonpost.com/news/wonk/wp/2015/01/06/the-u-s-has-more-jails-than-colleges-heres-a-map-of-where-those-prisoners-live/.

9 https://obamawhitehouse.archives.gov/the-press-office/2016/06/10/fact-sheet-white-house-launches-fair-chance-higher-education-pledge

10 https://www.gracechurchhonesdale.org/files/homilies/CriminalJusticeFactSheetNAACP.pdf

11 https://www.rand.org/pubs/research_reports/RR266.html

Fortnite vs. W.C. Franks—Millard Plaza, Circa 1980's
12 https://www.aps.org/publications/apsnews/200810/physicshistory.cfm

Reading Harry Potter and the Chamber of Secrets
13 Children's Literacy Foundation http://clifonline.org/resources/research/